A CURE OF DELINQUENTS

ALSO BY ROBERT SHIELDS

The Child's First Five Years

A CURE OF DELINQUENTS

The Treatment of Maladjustment

by

ROBERT W. SHIELDS, Ph.D.

HEINEMANN
LONDON

Heinemann Educational Books Ltd
LONDON EDINBURGH MELBOURNE TORONTO
AUCKLAND SINGAPORE JOHANNESBURG
HONG KONG NAIROBI IBADAN NEW DELHI

ISBN 0 435 80790 0

© Robert W. Shields, 1962, 1971
First published 1962
Second Edition 1971

Published by
Heinemann Educational Books Ltd
48 Charles Street, London W1X 8AH
Printed in Great Britain by Morrison and Gibb Ltd
London and Edinburgh

Contents

	Introduction by Dr D. W. Winnicott	7
	Foreword by Wilfred F. Kemp	9
	Preface to the Second Edition	11
	Preface to the First Edition	13
1	Approach	15
2	The School	23
3	Method	32
4	The Maladjusted Child	53
5	Discipline	63
6	Communication	78
7	Inter-Staff Tensions	85
8	Distrust of Psychotherapy	93
9	The Anti-Social Child	101
10	Psychotherapy and the Law	112
11	Theory and Practice	122
12	Clinical Observations	135
13	Etiology	146
14	Progress Report	151
15	Perspective	158
16	Recommendations	168
17	Conclusion	179
	Postscript	182
	Bibliography	183
	Index	189

To
Linda and Sonja

Introduction

by Dr D. W. Winnicott, F.R.C.P.

This book is a report by a psychotherapist on a London County Council experimental school for maladjusted boys. Bredinghurst was a school of considerable distinction because of its policy of providing management supplemented by psychotherapy; such a school may be called pioneer even though similar attempts have been and are being made elsewhere.

Robert Shields has attempted to do much more, however, than to make a report. He has set out his views on maladjustment and on the management of anti-social boys, and he has discussed both the theory and the inherent practical difficulties. Using his experience in the school, he has been able to write a highly informative account which in my opinion achieves a high place in the vast literature on this subject, one that calls urgently for new understanding.

The attempt to deal with anti-social children involves the general public, and especially those who take it upon themselves to represent the public in Parliament and on County Councils. This must be true because of the nature of the disorder from which these children suffer – and suffer they do. It is not a matter of simply making a diagnosis and providing a treatment; it is more that the child's condition forces society to react; and it is only if society is well informed that it can act in such a way that the outcome is favourable. What is needed is something that is neither sentimental nor revengeful.

A specialized environment is needed for these children in order that they may begin to reach to their own personal problems instead of compulsively seeking a solution in anti-social behaviour. Each child needs to experience the personal conflicts which were hidden in the original infantile setting by reactions to environmental failures. The psychotherapist plays his part in enabling the child to resolve the inner predicament which belongs to any child, whether anti-social or not.

In my personal opinion this book will be of great value to the general public and to committee members who are involved in and need to know what is going on in the schools that they serve and for which they take corporate responsibility. The author uses the work of Freud and makes acknowledgement to him and many other authors, but what he says is not in any way a re-hash of psycho-analytic theory. What he has to say is valuable to those engaged in the actual work but it is written in such a way that it can be understood by those whose special knowledge is in other fields.

The argument of the book hinges on the provision of psychotherapy in conjunction with school management, and for me it is most important that the author fully acknowledges his indebtedness to the teachers and the other members of the staff, without whose co-operation psychotherapy has no meaning. In combating the anti-social tendency the therapist works with all the others who are engaged in management and teaching. This book makes a real attempt to lay a basis for mutual understanding between the various professional groups who bring differing approaches to the task and who are probably of dissimilar temperaments.

It is exactly here, in the provision of therapy within the school setting, that the most hopeful work is being done towards a lessening of the numbers of delinquents or recidivists among the adults of our society.

D.W.W.

Foreword

by Wilfred F. Kemp, Headmaster Bredinghurst School, 1948-59

It was in 1943 that the Education Officer for Special Services, Colonel E. Eton, first talked with me about making 'boarding provision for problem children'. Together we agreed that evacuation hostels, run by me for the London County Council at Braughing in Hertfordshire, should take up to half their number of such cases. This work was extended under the administration of Mr G. A. N. Lowndes. It was his enthusiasm and concern for these children, by now classified under the 1944 Education Act as 'maladjusted', that furthered my interest. From discussions with him and the experience we gained over the next few years we saw the need for an all-embracing educational treatment centre for maladusted children.

Bredinghurst School was opened in 1948. Though we were enthusiastic, full of ideas, equipped with some knowledge and experience, it was nevertheless correctly called an experimental school. The limitations of a purely educational and environmental set-up had been exposed to me, but as an educator I was suspicious of psychiatry.

The appointment of Dr H. G. Williams as psychiatrist on the School Medical Officer's staff, with responsibility for Bredinghurst, was a most fortunate event. He was a man of immense kindliness and understanding, tolerant of other people's attitudes and opinions, and a good listener. Following his death in 1954 Dr James M. Taylor was appointed as the psychiatrist. A year after the school was opened, Dr R. W. Shields and Miss P. Winterbottom joined the staff. Thus a complete psychiatric unit – psychiatrist, psychotherapist, and psychiatric social worker – was integrated into the school. In addition, Miss M. Procter, our educational psychologist, attended one day each week.

A viable relationship and an unfettered understanding between the various disciplines represented on the staff was essential. My aim was to recruit individuals who could work amicably together – psychiatric, teaching, and child care. There had to be a friendly and enthusiastic interchange of opinions, ideas, knowledge, and observations between us, and from which we all could benefit. The manner in which individual psychotherapy dovetailed into the work of the school was in large measure due to the personality of Dr Shields. His patience, skill, and thoroughness continually impressed me and led to a smoothness of relationships between the psychiatric and educational sides of the school. In his book he explains the problems we had to cope with, the manner in which we set about the task, and what we learned in ten years of very close association. I would commend it as a most serious exercise to all those who have to deal with maladjusted children.

1962   W.F.K.

Preface to the Second Edition

Since this book was first published the climate of opinion in this country concerning the management and treatment of maladjusted and delinquent children has undergone a dramatic change. The personal and social problems such children pose are now commonly accepted as falling within the overall responsibility of the local authority and State-aided special education. Fortunately, though, this has not prevented independent schools, in which so often the pioneering work is done, from continuing their efforts in the same field. Though both educational and therapeutic provision for these children is still far from adequate, many new schools have been opened in various parts of the country, some of them purpose-built.

There is a widening interest among teachers and house-staff in the dynamic approach to treatment and a recognition that advanced training is called for if they are to equip themselves to work with an interdisciplinary team. In the schools themselves there is a greater appreciation of the essential role which the therapist has to play both in the actual treatment situation and in supporting the efforts of other staff members. The problem now is not that therapists are viewed with suspicion but that there are not enough therapists to meet the demand, and many headmasters find themselves unable to get the help they wish for.

Administratively also the situation is changing in that local authorities in some areas have appointed new permanent officers who have specialized knowledge of the maladjusted child, and some inspectors are ex-teachers who have themselves worked in school for the maladjusted child and so know the problem at first hand.

Not least among the influences which have brought about these changes in climate is that of the various training courses which have been established for teachers who wish to work with maladjusted children or delinquents. It gives me particular pleasure to select for mention the first-established course of this kind which was begun by my colleague, Dr Edna Oakeshott, at the London University Institute of Education in 1952. The work which she has pioneered has been of incalculable value in offering experienced teachers an advanced training for this type of work, and in generating an enlightened attitude to this form of specialism throughout the educational system. I have been most fortunate over the past ten years in having been co-tutor on this course.

1970   R.W.S.

Preface to the First Edition

Since the passing of the Children's Act in 1948 the London County Council has created a comprehensive and inter-locking organization for the treatment of emotionally disturbed children. In addition to the services provided by the paediatric departments of the main teaching hospitals there are now in existence seven Child Guidance Units which are maintained by the Public Health Department of the Council. Similarly the Education Department has made special provision for the maladjusted and delinquent child. Eighteen tutorial classes for children with personality or educational difficulties, three day schools for maladjusted children, and eight residential schools have been established.

This rapid development in special services for emotionally handicapped children has taken place under the administration of Dr Denis Pirrie, the Schools Medical Officer, Miss Dorothy A. Plastow, the Assistant Education Officer in charge of Special Schools, and Miss Margaret Procter, now the Council's Senior Educational Psychologist. The combined efforts of these officers of the Council have opened up a new field in social service and widened the scope for vigorous co-operation between complementary disciplines. Though Bredinghurst was the first school for maladjusted children in this country to incorporate into its structure a full psychiatric team, at the time of writing two other schools have adopted a similar pattern.

Every school is a reflection of the gifts and personality of the headmaster. Bredinghurst was fortunate in that for the first eleven years of its existence it had as its headmaster Mr Wilfred F. Kemp whose humanity, sensitivity, patience and tolerance made a vital contribution to the work outlined here.

I am particularly grateful to Mr Masud R. Khan for endless encouragement throughout the preparation of the manuscript, for his constructive and helpful criticism, and for many helpful suggestions which have been incorporated in the text.

My direct association with the London County Council's special education service will be apparent; but I should make it clear that any opinions or conclusions are my own.

1962   R.W.S.

I

Approach

Though strictly not interchangeable terms, there is a tendency to link maladjustment and delinquency. Delinquency always includes maladjustment, and most maladjusted children are at one time or another delinquent. Both conditions compel the environment to take an active role in handling, management, and cure. Both are the result of deprivation, acute or partial. Major problems arise not so much in diagnosis nor in observing the child's need for help of some kind, but in deciding on the kind of management or treatment to which the child will best respond.

Confusion arises in no small measure because the maladjusted child himself presents his predicament in three very different ways which have led to three different methods of treatment and of social attitude to the problem as a whole:

(1) *That the child has been diagnosed as maladjusted implies that his childhood environment has failed him (or he has failed it), and that active measures have to be taken to provide him with an alternative environment.* The child's obvious revolt against, or disturbance in, his home environment gave rise to the earliest experiments in reform and re-education. It is seldom difficult to detect in the home certain parental attitudes which might be considered inimical to healthy development: over-discipline, lack of discipline, cruelty, subtle sadistic pressures, low moral standards, insanity, parental disagreements or separations, incestuous relationships, and so on. It is possible to argue, therefore, that if the child's maladjustment stems from an inadequate environment the provision of a new and healthier environment may effect a cure. In addition, corrective teaching and high moral standards may serve to establish in the

child a new set of values to which he will find it convenient to conform.

Much work with disturbed children is still based upon this thesis, the hope being that the child will recognize, appreciate, and respond positively to this 'better' environment; that he will relinquish his neurotic patterns and ego distortions, and become socially conforming.

When he proves reluctant or unable to effect this change spontaneously direct pressure, both moral and social, is brought to bear upon him in the hope that he will find life more tolerable if he does conform, and extremely painful if he declines to do so.

Those who subscribe to this point of view place emphasis, naturally, upon re-education, punitive measures, and moral attitudes. A school based on these principles cultivates a rigid and systematic method. The child finds a firm and energetic programme outlined for him; his time is taken up in purposeful social activities, regular school hours, organized games, gardening, and 'projects' of all kinds. Any disinclination for these activities is seen by the staff as defiance, wilfulness, perversity, or evidence of persisting depravity. The child who will not mix or who spends his time dreaming or becomes withdrawn and depressed generates anxiety in the staff who feel that he ought to respond to the exciting and gregarious programme that has been mapped out for him. His 'progress' can be simply calculated by the variety and standards of the new skills he learns, and by the lack of friction between him and the staff members.

One could easily criticize this approach as unimaginative and lacking in insight, in spite of the fact that many re-educators nowadays give a veneer of sophistication to these methods by trying assiduously to incorporate modified psycho-analytical concepts. Their methods do, however, have much to commend them. All maladjusted children suffer from a sense of insecurity with varying degrees of intensity, and the organized rigidity of this type of environment acts as a reassurance, and can be understood and used by some children as loving concern.

The maladjusted child's personal fight against his inward chaos may easily seduce the school into providing him with a new environment which has only one virtue: an organized denial of this chaos. The external orderliness, confidence, and disciplinary firmness does much to reduce the child's personal anxiety and may, in favourable cases, give him a framework of security around which he can re-orientate himself. Such a school also makes fewer demands upon the staff in terms of intellectual awareness, emotional stress and anxiety. Not having to understand the intricate nature of the child's dependency patterns, and lacking any skill by which to examine the dynamics and consequent responsibilities of the transference relationship, the staff feel more free, less encumbered by the child's fantasies and emotional needs, and more able to apply themselves energetically but uncritically to comparatively simple tasks which appear to have obvious and measurable results.

One practical advantage of a school of this kind is that administrators are likely to be sympathetic towards it. Many schools are now run by local authorities and most are subject to some supervision by administrators, inspectors, or elected committees. Administrators, not being teachers or child-care specialists, are, not unnaturally, mostly concerned with the smooth running of a school. Generally they are favourably impressed by the school which is orderly, where the children are smartly dressed and well mannered, and where the classrooms and dormitories are neat and tidy. Administrators will mean it as a compliment, and some headmasters will take it as one, when they say: 'These children look and behave so normally that I would never have guessed it was a school for the maladjusted.'

Unfortunately this approach suffers from two serious disadvantages. It does not lead to conspicuously good results. Many children fail altogether to respond to what is offered them and the school lacks both the skill and resilience to make special provision for such children. Many others respond well so long as they are in the school, as though using the external framework to their advantage while they are still a part of it, but once they leave the school their symptoms return and old anti-social behaviour patterns re-assert themselves. Yet others become socially conforming and continue so after they leave but this social improvement is achieved only at great personal cost to themselves, super-ego formulations preventing the full development and employment of the total personality.

The second and more grave disadvantage is that since the system is based upon what can be done *for* the child and places virtually no emphasis upon understanding the psycho-dynamics of maladjustment, little knowledge is gained. When staffing these schools the administrators favour pure educationists, 'good disciplinarians', physical-training experts and handicraft teachers. Obviously there is a place for all these qualities and skills in a school. The fault lies not in what is included but in what is excluded.

Either no provision is made for psychiatric help in the school, or else the therapist's time is so restricted that adequate treatment is not possible. Psycho-analytical ideas and psychiatric personnel alike are felt to be threatening and inimical to the main purpose of the school. To look below the surface of the child's behaviour is to question the accepted principles upon which the school is functioning, and may weaken the conviction and impact of the disciplinary measures employed.

The unfortunate result is that, despite the clamant need for a therapeutic approach to delinquency, virtually no use is made of the wealth of research and clinical material that is available. Children come and go without anyone being able to discover the root cause of their emotional and social disturbance, or being able to state in what way the environment succeeded, or failed, in curing their condition. It is a sad reflection that, although schools and institutions of this type have been in existence for many generations, little or nothing of value has been published on their work which can throw light on the etiology of delinquency or furnish a convincing programme of remedial treatment.

(2) The maladjusted child does not draw the community's attention to himself solely by way of his delinquency or anti-social tendencies. He only evokes in the minds of more sensitive individuals a sense of his own unhappiness and distress. What we may perhaps call his *'gestural behaviour' indicates not only an external maladjustment but an inward disorder also.* Alongside his conflict with his environment he may show clear signs of inward distress, a large variety of personally painful symptoms indicating profound disillusionment with himself, educational retardation, depression, and gross lack of self-confidence.

Just as there are those who find it easy to respond to the anti-social attitudes in the young by disciplinary and moral techniques, so there are those whose compassion compels them to react to the inward misery of the maladjusted child by attempting to com-

APPROACH 19

pensate him for the wrongs, real or imagined, to which his earlier environment has exposed him.

Many schools and institutions exist which adopt the position that nothing will be gained merely by siding with the environment against the delinquent, and consequently the staff identify themselves with the child, persuading themselves that all he needs is love, patience, and tolerance. These schools make positive use both of the child's willingness to seek affection from mature adults and his ability to regress[1] to more primitive forms of dependence. The child, from a new-found conviction of the adult world's capacity for compassion and kindliness, may then slough off his anti-social poses and adopt more positive attitudes to life.

It would not be difficult to criticize this approach as being oversentimental, yet the fact remains that very many children do grasp at this 'second chance', are able to correct their earlier emotional bias against the community and become normally healthy adults. Although such schools have been ridiculed as 'love is enough' institutions, many of them can rightly claim to have been the vehicle by which dramatic changes have been effected in the life of many a child.

A number of legitimate criticisms can be advanced against this method. The first is that, in the main, institutions that adopt this approach give the impression of almost unlimited chaos. In some there is no regular schooling whatever, educational instruction being given only when the child himself asks for it. This disturbs the educationalist who, naturally enough, feels that formal education is so necessary a part of the child's equipment that it should not be left entirely to individual whim. Since the staff in these schools place great store upon the value of regressive modes of behaviour in the child, discipline is lax, there is a minimum of adult-directed orderliness, anti-social behaviour tends to be excused or overlooked, delinquency appears to be condoned, and adult rights and points of view are largely subordinated to those of the child. All these factors generate great anxiety in the minds of observers and administrators alike. It has also to be admitted that schools of this type make excessively heavy demands upon the physical and emotional reserves of the staff, and consequently many of them are unsettled and stay only a short time.

1. The capacity on the part of the patient to resort to childish or infantile moods, behaviour patterns and emotional attitudes.

One significant advantage this approach has over the first is that it does give the child the opportunity to demonstrate how disturbed he really is. Disciplinary techniques strengthen the child's own defences against his emotional illness and may only serve to disguise his true predicament. The more lax environment goes, perhaps, to the opposite extreme and seems to suggest that manifest evidence of an inward disorganization is not only tolerated but is an absolute good. Once this state is reached the school provides reassurance, techniques for the avoidance of anxiety, and sustained affection. Clinical work shows, however, that mere reassurance and the elimination of anxiety are not in themselves always therapeutic, and affective processes without insight may actively militate against therapeutic and developmental processes.

It is possible to argue that in this type of institution we see again the delinquent's ability to seduce the environment to respond to one side only of his need and problem. At some stage in his infantile development the delinquent has suffered an actual or fantasied failure in love. It is equally true that the majority of delinquents do react favourably to affectionate and tolerant attitudes on the part of adults, often showing delicate and touching gestures of gratitude. Nevertheless, so long as the adult worker lacks understanding of the intra-psychic processes which led to failure in the initial home-situation, he will find himself seduced by the delinquent into repeating exactly the same kind of failure in this later context. So long also as the delinquent himself gains no insight into his affective predicament, he will use the new environment only to reinforce his own conviction of having been betrayed or misunderstood.

It is these mechanisms which lead so many workers who rely upon compassion alone to become disillusioned and embittered through repeated failures and disappointments.

(3) The delinquent mobilizes the attention of the environment by revealing that *he is the victim of unconscious intra-psychic forces within himself*. It is this aspect of the problem which appeals to the therapist, for example at a Child Guidance Clinic. By using the transference[2] situation to lay bare and make available to

2. By 'transference' is meant the development of an emotional attitude on the part of the patient towards one or more adults, an attitude which reflects

interpretation the original psychic conflict, the therapist hopes it will be possible for the child to gain insight into the manner in which he contributes to his present predicament (by perpetuating infantile patterns) and so help him to relinquish his anti-social attitudes.

While having very obvious advantages this method suffers from one crippling disadvantage: it does not provide a setting in which the child can be held while treatment is taking place. Treatment has to be offered while the child is still in the home, in the environment in which the initial breakdown took place and which is generally quite incapable of sufficient adaptability or resilience to withstand the stresses that treatment will impose.

It is for this reason that while Child Guidance Clinics are remarkably successful in treating minor neurotic disturbances in the young they are so ineffectual in treating severe maladjustment and delinquency. It has to be added, also, that the therapist working in a Child Guidance Unit is easily held to ransom by the fecklessness of the child's parents, or by their blunt refusal to co-operate.

It must have been considerations of this kind that led the London County Council to attempt the imaginative experiment of incorporating a full psychiatric unit in a school for maladjusted children, thus bringing into close association teachers, child-care staff, and a psychiatric team. Although all of us who took part in this experiment and worked together for upwards of a decade are fully convinced that it was an eminently worthwhile piece of work, it must not be thought that inter-disciplinary relationships were always easy and harmonious.

To the obvious difficulties of this kind of association between individuals with vastly diverse trainings, points of view and experience, must be added the fact that maladjusted children have a singular capacity for sensing and exploiting disagreements between adult members of the staff. It is possible that the very nature of the work with delinquent children is so fraught with anxiety, with complicated patterns of transference and counter-transference, and exceptional forms of responsibility that smooth staff relationships

---

and reproduces much earlier feelings (both of love and hate) which originally characterized his feelings for his parents.

are an unattainable ideal. Nevertheless the rich rewards of the work itself and the exceptional opportunity for widening one's personal experience and knowledge through this association are more than ample compensation for occasional personal discomfitures.

2

The School

BREDINGHURST SCHOOL in Peckham, a district of South London, does not stand in extensive grounds but the various buildings are well planned and laid out. In a semi-circle around the central building, which comprises the main classrooms, administrative offices, and headmaster's accommodation, are set the three houses, known as 'cottages', in which the children live. On the other side of the central building are two large playing-fields and a fourth house which contains another classroom and the rooms used by the psychotherapist and psychiatric social worker. Each of the boys' cottages is a separate unit, catering for the complete needs of fifteen boys, with separate cooking facilities and with its own staff living in alongside the boys. The two junior cottages have women staff while in the senior cottage a married couple is in charge. The premises as a whole have a pleasing appearance. The gardens are attractive and carefully tended. All furniture is of good quality, and internal decorations tastefully done in cheerful colours. Every effort has been made to avoid giving the impression of an 'institution' and the cottages themselves have a homely 'lived-in' atmosphere – clean without being obsessionally so, tidy without being meticulously ordered. There is colour, warmth and comfort, without luxury or lavish expenditure. The school is within easy reach of bus and train, and within a few miles are several parks and Green-Belt woodlands.

The health of the children has always been good. Their physical well-being has high priority, no child being deprived of the normal care which a good home would provide. In all cases the school assumes the responsibility for ensuring that the boys are properly and warmly clothed; parents who cannot afford to do this pay a small token sum towards the cost of clothing provided by the Council. If even this small sum cannot be found by the parents the

Council meets the entire cost. Catering is carefully planned and on a generous scale. Food is bought in bulk, but each house-mother is free to prepare it as she wishes and vary the menu to suit herself.

The fact that the school exists in a densely populated area of London demands that a good relationship be maintained between it and the local community. Complaints from residents, shop-owners, and police are dealt with promptly and every attempt is made to keep the boys under reasonable control. It might be considered a simpler expedient, for this reason alone, to locate a school of this type in the country where as well as the population being sparse the temptations for the delinquent, in theory at least, would be considerably reduced. The majority of schools for maladjusted children are, in fact, in the country. In our view, however, the arguments in favour of this arrangement are outweighed by other considerations.

The boys we are commissioned to treat are city-born and -bred. They are accustomed to crowds, to dense traffic, to urban sights and sounds, to blocks of flats, and to walking on concrete. Furthermore this is the environment to which they will eventually return. To accommodate the maladjusted child in a country school is to create for him a certain air of unreality, of detachment from home and familiar things which are so much a part of his personality framework. To accustom him to a rural environment may be as difficult a process as to get him used again, at the end of his stay, to the urban setting from which the rest of the family have never been removed.

More important, if a child is drastically detached from his home geographically, the artificial change of environment might yield a first quick gain in 'recovery-symptoms' which, while impressive to the casual observer, would not be enduring. Omnipotent handling of the situation by drastically interfering with the accustomed environment may be no more than a trap, for the child's own omnipotent gestures are a very large part of his primitive strivings and it only leads to confusion and distortion of the problem if we blindly identify ourselves with them.

When the school is located in the city, by contrast, no dramatic dissociation has taken place in relation to the total environment and it is possible to maintain a very close link between home and school. The social workers and other members of the staff can, without delay or difficulty, visit the home of any child and a meaningful contact can be sustained between the parents, the child, and the school personnel. There is a sustained and easy flow of information. News of small but significant domestic events which may be of great consequence to the child quickly reaches the school, and the cost of travel either way is insignificant. Parents can visit their child with ease should he become ill or should their own anxieties and concern compel them to call. Regular week-end leave also makes it possible for the child to keep in close touch with his family.

When a school is at a great distance from the child's home it encourages the kind of parent who is only too eager to hand over his responsibilities, to cut himself off completely from all knowledge and communication with the child. Just as it is vitally important for the boy to keep the memory of his parents alive within himself, so it is important that his parents should not allow him and his needs to fall into the backgrounds of their minds. The geographical and emotional complications which inevitably arise when a school is established in the country must diminish to a very considerable degree this mutual fostering of memory and sentiment.

Not least among the advantages of having the school close to the homes of the children is that the boy who is excessively anxious or depressed, and feels compelled from time to time to run away from the school, has little difficulty in finding his way home:

> Arthur's mother had for several years suffered from a severe heart condition which he knew might at any time result in her death. To be away from her for any length of time inevitably set his his mind worrying about her. There were so many things he could do for her if he were at home which would ease her physical burden and so prolong her life. The longer he was away from home the more convinced he became that his absence was having an adverse effect on her health and he would torment himself with the notion that she had died, alone, and without his having had an opportunity to say good-bye to her. By the Wednesday of each week Arthur's face took on a strained look. Classwork was clearly impossible for him because his mind was filled with anxious foreboding about his mother. He felt guilty lest, by not being there to help her, he had compelled her to overtax her limited strength. If she were to die the blame would be his.
>
> He *had* to go home. He *had* to be reassured that she was still alive, that she could survive without the benefit of his physical strength. Over a period of several months he ran away regularly from school

in mid-week and walked straight home just to assure himself that all was well and to assist his mother in the necessary home chores.

Had the school been deep in the country it would have been extremely difficult for him to reach home and to reassure himself that all was well. The guilt, anxiety, and nervous strain to which he would have been subjected might have proved insupportable.

Quite apart from geography it is the deliberate policy at Bredinghurst to keep the child's link with his family intact in so far as it is possible. It is a maxim of Child Guidance Work that a clinic cannot adequately treat a boy in a vacuum: he can only be understood as a whole person when he is seen in the setting of the family unit. This is our maxim also. The total social problem, as well as the actual predicament of the individual child, needs to be kept constantly in fine focus. Unless this can be done and the wider family problem kept in view much conscientious and sensitive work will be wasted. It is not possible to see the whole child so long as one sees only the child. The interdependence of the child, the family, and the school is the matrix upon which the fabric of therapy is constructed.

Bredinghurst is not a mental hospital, though it has many features in common with such a hospital. It is, first and foremost, a school. The headmaster has the immediate responsibility and all administration falls on his shoulders. Though great emphasis is placed upon the psychiatric orientation of the school and certain concessions are made to therapeutic needs and aims, the normal educational programme is never ignored. This emphasis on the educational aspect seeks to endorse the basic health in the child and his nearness to normality. To stress the 'hospital' aspect of treatment would, in our view, be to cut these children off from the kind of free life a child enjoys and which keeps intact his links with normality and everyday living.

It is valuable, therefore, to bear in mind that the maladjusted child has not yet achieved the rigid status of an ill human-being. He is more 'open', more fluid, and in a transitional state between health and ill-health. Maladjustment in this sense is not so much a symptom or an illness as a groping towards health or illness. It seems to be at exactly this point that most analytical work with disturbed children goes astray. The clinician looks at the maladjusted child as a neurotic and studies his purely internal conflicts, which assume a clear-cut characterological configuration. But in certain ways the maladjusted child has not yet established a firm and definable territory of 'me-ness'. The self and the primary environment are still fused and only gradually become separated out. Maladjustment reflects both these processes – differentiation and maintenance of fusion. Hence the environment has to reflect both a resilience towards the specific needs of the maladjusted child and at the same time provide a true and concrete sample of external reality.

The school offers a certain basic pattern, a substratum of cohesion and discipline tied into a normal though elastic social and educational scheme. To attempt always to adhere strictly to a rigid educational programme would, nevertheless, not take into full account the personal difficulties and limitations of the individual child. Most maladjusted children are generally well behind their peers in educational attainment. Anxiety lowers the threshold of learning. Deep concern with inward tensions prevents full and unfettered concentration upon outward and impersonal studies. Specific emotional difficulties produce specific learning blockages. In Bredinghurst, therefore, the classes are small, thereby enabling the teacher to give individual attention to each child. Once a child has made enough progress in school work to make it possible for him to fit into an ordinary class, and his behaviour is no longer grossly disturbed, he is sent to an 'outside school'. By this is meant, quite simply, that he attends an ordinary day school in the locality but continues to live at Bredinghurst as if it were his home.

Many delinquent and maladjusted children are of low or low-average intelligence. With them the aim must be to see that what progress can be reasonably expected will be made. At the other end of the scale there is to be found the boy of exceptionally high intelligence who may use his above-average mind as a means of flight from inner emotional conflict. Over-intellectualization can be as disastrous to the personality, as emotionally inhibiting, as great a threat to personal integration, as distorting to emotional attitudes, as can obvious disturbance and overt delinquency.

In such cases it must be considered as part of the educational programme to slow down deliberately the pace of learning and thus give the child space and time in which to fall inwards upon himself and find, when in a receptive mood, some real contact with his own complicated psychic structure and emotional ambivalences. This slowing-down can thus make toleration by the child of depressive moods possible. Many children use intellectual development as a manic defence against their depressive feelings just as some others employ anti-social acts as a defence mechanism. Unusually severe demands are bound to be made upon the teacher in such an environment. While remaining a pedagogue he must, nevertheless, be willing to accept and adapt himself to unusual emotional needs, behaviour, pace and rhythm in his pupils. It is not always easy, for example, for a teacher who appreciates the responsive and intelligent student to see that an intense programme of advanced study may be impoverishing and distorting to the personality of the child – particularly when that teacher works in a school where low educational attainment on the part of the majority of his pupils must inevitably be felt as a very real personal frustration.

Despite what has just been said it is necessary, however, to provide a firm educational regime to which each boy is expected, within his recognized limitations, to conform. That from time to time he may be unable to do this will be tacitly admitted by the teaching staff; but this personal difficulty cannot be endlessly pampered. Nor can it, in my view, justify the notion that there should be no disciplinary programme whatsoever – the pupil dictating his own rate of learning and relying on no more than an occasional whim for scholarship. For the educationist to permit such a course would merely be to establish an unprofitable collusion between the administration and the boy's revolt against society, convention, normal discipline, and reality.

We observed earlier that the chief danger of treating these children in remote country schools is that it leads to a split in the child's personality. The avoidance of discipline is another example of splitting which the child might abuse as a collusion on the part of the school with his magical and omnipotent fantasies. Perhaps here we may underline the need to differentiate between meeting the child's real needs and sentimentally colluding with his magical attempts at escape from pressures and conflicts that are inherent to human development. The teacher has to steer a difficult course between a rigid, inelastic educational programme and a weak and sentimental pose in which he surrenders his status as a teacher to make undue concession to the child's emotional disturbance.

The fundamental educational problem in this setting may be

defined as that of resolving the tensions that exist between the traditional role of the pedagogue with those of the compassionate humanitarian in the classroom who is acutely aware of the exceptional internal stresses to which his pupils are subject. This tension is, as I shall detail later, exacerbated by the fact that psychological treatment, with all its concomitant disturbances, is carried out in the school and during school hours. It necessarily implies that the teacher has to contend with occasional moods, emotional crises, and behavioural difficulties in his classroom which the teacher in an ordinary school is not called upon to meet.

The responsibilities of the residential staff, the house-fathers and house-matrons, may very broadly be equated with those of the nursing staff in a hospital. It is impossible to conceive that any worthwhile result could be achieved in a school of this calibre if the house-staff felt that their obligations towards the children were limited merely to seeing that they were well fed, well clothed, and kept clean, warm and comfortable – not that these things are unimportant. A very large proportion of the child's day is spent in the 'cottage' where he is in the care of the house-staff. It is they who wake him in the morning, supervise his washing, dressing, bed-making, meals, spare-time activities, hobbies, and preparations for bed. If he runs away from school it is, as often as not, their job to fetch him back and rehabilitate him into the cottage again. If he cannot sleep, or if he wakes terrified from a nightmare, it is they who comfort and reassure him.

Inevitably the house-staff take over in very large measure the parental role. It is to them that the child will be likely to feel the closest attachment, and it is from them he will demand the most intense and sustained care and sympathy. Without humanity, tolerance and resilience on the part of the house-staff, no real letting-go and relaxing of his rigid defensive attitudes can take place, for it is with them that he is most inclined to 'act-out' his personal conflicts with his parents. The house-staff will be the objects of his love and hate. From them he will demand comfort in depression, reassurance when anxious, and forgiveness when repentant.

The problem which the house-staff have to face is complicated in that they must keep order and reasonable discipline in the cottage while at the same time being able to tolerate bizarre behaviour in one boy or another who is going through an emotional crisis or is in a mood of blind anger or revolt. They need to be able to see and make allowance for the idiosyncrasies of the individual child while at the same time preserving a sense of family unity among the group. They must find ways of employing discipline that take into account the needs and capacities of the individual, yet not allow over-permissiveness to undermine the general stability of the cottage. While accepting without anxiety the role of parenthood, they cannot favour one child to the exclusion of another, nor can they assume the role of a parent in such a way as to interfere with the child's attachment to his own parents and his own home. It is essential that they be able to combine a warm humanity with the ability to understand the emotional problem lying at the back of the child's behaviour and misbehaviour. They need to be able to accept devotion without becoming possessive, hatred without taking umbrage, indecency without being outraged, and violence without being afraid.

To create, without obvious artifice, a genuine family feeling within the cottage is far from easy, but without this no real dependence can be felt by the child, nor will there be an adequate atmosphere of security and maternal kindliness in which alone there can be a true surrender to the inner emotional needs and conflicts from which his conscious actions and defiances have isolated him.

Inevitably the cost of administering a school of this calibre, which provides so many and varied services for a small number of children, is high. Not only must ordinary teaching services be provided, but the school must also feed, house and, usually, clothe everybody. In addition, the relatively high cost of employing skilled psychiatric staff has to be superimposed upon that of the residential-school expenses. Some parents are not in a position to pay much towards the cost of their child's keep and treatment. Others, bitterly resenting that their boy has been removed from home under a court order, decline to make any contribution whatever.

In my view this is an unsatisfactory state of affairs. Not to allow parents who can afford a considerable sum to pay fees commensurate with their income is only to support the natural anxiety of so many parents that the school designs to filch the child from their home and needlessly limits normal parental responsibility. Over and above this consideration is the fact that the more sensitive parent suffers from a deep sense of failure in regard to his child. If he is allowed to contribute as much as he is able to the boy's treatment it gives him opportunity to make some restitution to the child and to society, and thus decreases his feelings of guilt.

In our culture the state and the local authority have already taken over the normal parental functions to an astonishing degree with a consequent weakening of family dependencies and responsibilities to the detriment of the child. The smallest gesture of good faith and active concern which the parents of maladjusted children can reasonably be expected to make is that they should contribute financially as much as they can afford towards the cost of their child's treatment and physical care.

3
Method

Our aim at Bredinghurst has been to provide a special setting which will permit the child to relax his unconscious emotional defences in the framework of a therapeutic environment which is aware of and able to cater for his needs, while at the same time making near-normal educational and social demands on him, and ensuring that he (and the work-team) keeps in close contact with his own home.

This is the ideal picture, but to blend without undue strain and friction these very divergent skills, personalities, and points of view is no mean task. Much more than mere good will is needed from each member of the staff if anything resembling co-ordination of effort is to be achieved. It would be to create a false impression if one were to suggest that throughout the eleven years here under review all the members of the staff found easy agreement with one another. There were many differences of opinion, open criticisms, and personal tensions. Fortunately, however, a great measure of tolerance and understanding existed among the various professional staff as well as genuine friendship.

These qualities are not enough in themselves to bring about positive teamwork. There must be a common premise if any useful and concerted attack upon a problem is to be made. At Bredinghurst this premise has been that *maladjustment is just as much a response to inner drives and outer stimuli as is any other kind of human conduct, and that the ultimate aim of the school must be to cure and not merely contain.* These propositions are by no means universally held. Not a few of those who have at one time or other worked at Bredinghurst and very many administrators and educationalists look upon delinquency merely as a moral blind-spot which can be corrected by instruction or by religious appeal, and upon maladjustment as not more than an oddity of personality.

The personal tragedy of the deprived, depressed, maladjusted, or delinquent child is that the form his emotional malaise takes is one which very seldom endears him to society or makes an easy appeal to charity and compassion in others. Before admission to the school he will have been variously described as 'impossible', 'beyond control', 'affectionless', 'a disturbing influence on the whole school', 'slovenly, dirty-minded, disobedient, and unmanageable', 'a bed-wetter, a thief, and an unconscionable liar'. He may be truculent, violent, aggressive, resentful, rude, distrustful, utterly unreliable. Unpleasant character traits constitute his reply and reaction to a long experience of combat with environmental and family strictures. Within an emotionally disturbed setting he has built up a complex internal world of his own, designed to preserve him from the severe impact of hurtful factors in his environment and reduce his personal sense of pain.

Our first information concerning a child will consist of reports and impressions from day-school teachers, psychiatrists at Child Guidance Units, educational psychologists, or others who have at various times had dealings with the child. On the basis of these reports, which are sent to the school via one or other of the London Problem Cases Conferences, the headmaster decides whether or not he will admit a child. Once admission has been decided upon the psychiatric social worker visits the boy's home and makes the initial contact with the parents and the child. Much depends upon this visit.

Many parents are openly hostile. They may feel that they have betrayed their own child by having taken him to court as beyond control. They may, conversely, nurture a deep hatred for the 'Council' for having, under a Fit Person Order, assumed responsibility for their child. They may be tired of, and resentful towards, the many social workers, child welfare officers and probation officers who visit them from time to time, and our social worker may be considered to be just one more bureaucratic interloper. In such an atmosphere it is never easy, and may indeed prove impossible, for her to convince the parents that she has no wish to pry destructively or critically into their private lives. Many parents tend to look upon the social worker as an agent for the prosecution whose sole purpose is to indict them, to highlight their failures and condemn them for their errors. Since the majority of parents, particularly the more sensitive mothers, already suffer from an overwhelming sense of failure and despair about their child, merely to add to their guilt and depression would achieve nothing.

The social worker's first endeavour is to win the confidence of the boy and of his parents and persuade them that the school has only goodwill towards them. She explains in simple terms the physical setup, the methods of discipline, the system of privileges, and, above all, she invites the parents to ally themselves with the school in the treatment of their child. She invites them to visit the school before the child is admitted and to meet the headmaster, and she assures them that it is no part of our intention to entice the boy from his home or cut across his natural attachment to his parents. Not a small part of this interview is taken up in establishing a link with the child himself, who may be fearful, suspicious, or frantic with apprehension. Throughout the boy's stay in the school the social worker will remain in equally close touch with both the boy and his home. Sympathetic handling of this initial interview goes a long way towards lessening parental anxiety.

Not all parents are hostile. It frequently happens that the social worker is accepted as a friend and confidant of the family, or she may be welcomed because the parents believe they can dictate to her how their child should be handled – 'What he needs is a good taste of army discipline! None of this namby-pamby stuff the clinic have been dishing out!' – and she may be given an account of the ways in which other social agencies have wrongly handled the problem.

Child care officers and psychiatrists have often drawn attention to the lack of co-operation and insight evinced by the parents of delinquent and maladjusted children. This fact, they claim, frequently vitiates therapeutic work with exactly that type of home which could most benefit from the specialized services. Many of the homes from which our children are drawn are of this type: parents with very low intelligence; parents who are themselves delinquent; parents who are, clinically speaking, mad; parents who totally reject the child or cannot disguise their intense hatred of him.

Our major problem may not be how to treat the child, but how to keep him in treatment against the wishes of his parents. Many homes preserve a precarious emotional balance among the other members of the family by making a scapegoat of one child. There is a familial investment in this child's illness, and successful treatment constitutes a threat to the rest of the family. In such circumstances parents unconsciously work against the therapeutic process, occasionally with disastrous results:

> David L., soon after his admission, appeared before the juvenile court three times in three months. He had started treatment with me, had made a strong positive transference and was showing signs of improvement. On his third appearance at court, however, the magistrates were inclined to send him to an approved school but, as a result of our appeal, decided to return him to the school but put him on probation.
>
> From David's point of view, and ours, this was an unfortunate decision since it meant that if he ran away from school, even though he did not steal, his probation officer could charge him with breaking his probation. Unfortunately this is exactly what happened. Before the case was to be heard again David's mother told us that she was going to ask the court to allow him to return home. We pointed out that this was a fruitless plea and that, if she insisted on it, we felt that the magistrates would be likely to send her boy to an approved school and thus end his chances of getting the concentrated treatment he needed. We also emphasised that we were confident of his progress and eventual recovery.
>
> The case was heard by two magistrates who had not been at the earlier hearings and who asked the therapist to give his impressions. I pointed out that the probation order had put David in a cleft-stick. He could either abide by the conditions of his probation and not run away, or he could respond to the therapeutic environment and, in running away, show his trust in the school's capacity to get him back and to care sufficiently for him not to reject him.
>
> The magistrates accepted this point and decided not only to return David to Bredinghurst but also to set aside the probation order. The case seemed closed, and to the boy's advantage. At this point, however, his mother made her plea for the child to be returned home and the Fit Person Order set aside. On the surface this might have appeared to be the affectionate appeal of a devoted mother. In fact it was yet another expression of her basic hostility to her son. Exactly as we had predicted, the magistrates decided to reverse the decision made a few minutes earlier and to send David to an approved school.

This incident shows what difficulties can arise to complicate the therapeutic process when the school is faced with markedly ambivalent[1] attitudes on the part of parents. It also demonstrates how much thought, affectionate regard and skilled treatment on the part of the staff may be wasted by this kind of fiat.

Once a boy has been admitted he is immediately assigned to a cottage. Together with his parents he is free to talk with the headmaster, his teacher, and his house-mother. The parents are shown where their child will sleep and have an opportunity to inform the staff of his food-fads, particular anxieties, likes and dislikes. This style of introduction is important because it emphasises that the school is not a regulation boarding-school in which the duty of the child is to conform to a rigid and long-established régime, but that he is an individual being placed in an environment which largely resembles that of a good home.

Another boy of about his own age is usually delegated to look after the new entrant for the first few days and to acquaint him with the routine of the school. When his parents have taken their farewells the new boy is permitted to spend the rest of the day in the cottage and is not immediately thrust into the classroom. He may sit dejectedly in the cottage or, more usually, choose to attach himself to one of the women staff and follow her around, in much the same way as he might accompany and assist his mother with her household chores. By the time the first day is over he has generally made real contact with one or more of the women staff, knows several of the other boys by name, and feels relatively at ease. From the next day onwards he is expected to attend class. Since the classes are numerically small it is possible for him to be given individual care and tuition.

The new entrant is discussed at the school conference within a week or two of admission. At this initial conference the social worker outlines the boy's problem, details his previous history and treatment, and gives her impressions of the parents and the general home background. Her word-picture of the home provides a clear and incisive, though sympathetic, delineation of the conditions and pressures with which the child has had to contend. The case history is as complete as possible and is carried back to the child's

1. 'Ambivalence' is a psycho-analytical term used to connote the simultaneous existence in the individual of contradictory emotions (love and hate) towards the same person.

birth, nursing, infancy, and school experiences. Following this the cottage-staff are invited to give their impressions of his behaviour and initial reactions to the school, the staff and the other boys. The class-teacher by now has also made some estimate of the boy's scholastic attainments and of his emotional adjustment to the pupils in his group.

This résumé is deliberately designed merely as an introduction. No serious attempt is made at this point to determine the nature of the psychiatric problem, though it may not be difficult to arrive at a tentative diagnosis. The essential purpose of this conference is to permit each member of the staff who has so far had any dealings with the child to contribute towards an overall picture of the boy and his home which will be of value to the specialist staff who have yet to acquaint themselves at first-hand with the boy himself.

During the next fortnight the new boy is seen by the educational psychologist who not only arrives at an estimate of his Intelligence Quotient but also makes a report on the child's reaction to the testing situation, his willingness to co-operate, his obvious anxieties, and his personality. The child is also interviewed by our consultant psychiatrist.

At another conference, which takes place a week or two later, the same boy is discussed in much greater detail, the reports of the educational psychologist and the psychiatrist providing the chief points for discussion. It is the responsibility of the psychiatrist to arrive at a diagnosis, to outline what he considers to be the special difficulties with which the staff are likely to meet, to make a tentative prognosis, and finally to advise on whether or not the boy is likely to benefit from psychotherapy. It is not always possible for each child recommended for psychotherapy to receive it immediately, though the percentage of children under treatment is always high. But if it is felt that the need for treatment is urgent he may have his first session with the therapist the following day.

It may seem from the foregoing that within a few weeks of admission we have a clear picture of the total psychiatric, social and educational problem, and know to a nicety what the boy is like so that we can predict with accuracy how he will react and what progress he will make. This is not true of course. So far we have done little more than review with great care what is known of the child and his background. The picture we thus piece together may prove to be accurate but it is not much more than a conglomeration of impressions. There has, as yet, been little opportunity to discern the nature of the child's peculiar problem and personality configuration because he has not had time to establish a transference relationship.

It is impossible to overestimate the importance we place on the regular weekly conference in which all staff participate and are free to raise any query or air any opinion. Staff discussions, when they are open and adult, help to bring about a mood of self-examination while at the same time stimulating an enquiring attitude of mind. It has been our experience that virtually all workers have used the conference both as a method by which anxieties can be reduced through understanding of the psychic problems the children present and also as a medium and opportunity for analysing their own reactions and emotional attitudes to their work. It enables them to learn much about the kind of task on which they are engaged, about the qualities and personalities of their colleagues, and to gain a more complete picture of the boys under dicussion than they would separately be able to gain by personal observation. Thus the conference has become a useful form of training for new staff-members as well as serving its original purpose of pooling experience and information.

A superficial observer, if he were to see the boys only during their first few months in the school, might easily come to the conclusion that none of them is maladjusted. Each boy is well aware that he has been placed at Bredinghurst because he has in some way failed to match up to the demands of school and home, and he may at first make every effort to show that he is docile, well-behaved and tractable. It may be some months before he feels sufficiently secure in the goodwill and understanding of the staff to slough off his façade and reveal the complicated nature of his inner problem, and test the new environment.

The boy, for example, who is terrified of dependence upon others cannot feel safe until he has tested out the quality and sincerity of the personalities of the staff. Until he has started to convince himself of their capacity to bear with him in every mood and to identify themselves with his unconscious drives and fears, he may appear to be a perfectly healthy, sociable child. But once the stage has been reached where real dependence is possible his behaviour is likely suddenly to deteriorate. He now feels safe enough not to have to disguise his hatred, his fears, his sudden tempers, his feelings of jealousy, his intense need for love. He will become defiant, will perhaps run away again and again, may become delinquent and difficult to control.

Not the least important quality in the staff at Bredinghurst is that they have learned not to be misled by the initial docile phase, and have come to recognize that wild behaviour and truanting may be signs of a positive attachment to the staff and not a rejection of them, a note of hope and not of despair.

>Tony, aged ten, came to us after being turned out of six previous schools on account of his impossible behaviour. His father, a demolition worker, was a near-delinquent with no understanding of his children and little affection for them. His mother, while being able to love and show tenderness towards Tony's twin brother, preserved a strange attitude of detachment and distaste for Tony himself. She freely admitted to our social worker that, while she could recognize many good points in Tony's character and was impressed by his constant attentions towards her and his obvious devotion, she was unable to feel any affection for him. She had never been able to hold him in her arms, to cuddle or comfort him, and whenever he had attempted to climb on her lap she was seized with an irresistible revulsion and invariably thrust him away.

During the first week or two at Bredinghurst Tony appeared to get on well with everyone and was no particular problem in the school or cottage. The only remarkable thing about him was his head-banging at night: he would strike his head with sickening force against the wall by his bed for an hour or so at a time. He was accepted for treatment from the start and used his time with me in a friendly manner, talking of his home and interests in a singularly adult and detached, though guarded, manner.

Before long, however, he began to have uncontrollable outbursts of anger for no obvious reason. In these moods he would do extremely dangerous things, such as climbing and running on the roof of the school or cottage, or climbing to the topmost branches of the trees in the grounds. Many times he narrowly escaped falls which would probably have been fatal. It was exactly this kind of behaviour that had led to his expulsion from his previous schools and he clearly expected to meet the same type of rejection from us.

When he discovered that this idea was never entertained by the school, and his fear had been interpreted to him by the therapist in terms of his past experiences, his compulsive climbing gradually ceased and an element of depression crept into his outbursts of rage. Now he would cry when he was angry, and when upset would threaten to run away. Once or twice he did leave the school grounds but stayed nearby as though afraid that if he went too far no one would bother to fetch him back.

One afternoon when I was in my room alone a stone crashed through the window, scattering broken glass over me and the desk. I went outside and found Tony standing on the lawn with an armful of stones. These he was throwing at anyone who ventured near. I walked towards him and said: 'I guess I know how you feel, Tony.' He was weeping and screaming, all at the same time. He warned me: 'Don't come any nearer if you value your life. . . . I'm going to run away and you're not going to stop me.' I said: 'You're right, I'm not going to stop you. But I want you to know that I appreciate your letting me know how you feel; and if you do run away, we shall be glad to see you when you come back. . . .' His only rejoinder was to call me 'a bloody bugger', and with that he dropped the remainder of the stones and nimbly climbed over the fence and was gone.

Late that night he returned. When next he came to see me he made some light-hearted comment on my shattered window and then curled himself up on the rug by the fire. After sighing heavily a few times he began to cry, with his face averted. I could see the tears falling on to the carpet. He sobbed silently for the rest of the hour and was quite unable to say anything.

The following session he came into my room and sat on the edge of the chair opposite me. Leaning forward he thrust his head in his hands and began to make sucking noises with spittle between his teeth, and to dribble on the floor. He also rocked himself back and forward on the chair and made clicking sounds in his throat. I linked this up with his need to experience being a baby in a secure environment and to establish it in the transference as a valid experience.

In less time than it takes to tell he leant back on the hard wooden chair, let his head fall over the back-rest, and was fast asleep.

He slept soundly for the rest of the hour and when I woke him gently he thrust balled-up fists in his eyes in the manner of a small child waking. Then, trying to stand, he found his legs give way under him, so he crawled on the floor for a few moments before getting up and taking his leave. His treatment had begun.

Tony was able to go to sleep only because he knew I could hold in focus both the regressive and aggressive elements in his nature. He could sleep in the analytical setting because he was unconsciously aware that I was in touch with the aggressive side of his character and was able to wait for it and hold it. True regression is possible only where the patient can take for granted the therapist's realization that the passive mood runs side by side with the aggressive mood and that both are acceptable to the therapist. Tony knew that I was aware he would not always be passive as a result of being able to sleep, but that he would gradually wake to an intensely aggressive attitude which had new meaning and dimension because the therapist could keep in touch with both elements:

> For many sessions following this Tony went to sleep during the analytic hours, sleeping either in his chair or after rolling himself up tightly in the carpet like a child in swaddling clothes. Gradually, however, he chose to sleep nearer and nearer to my chair till he was using my foot as a pillow. Later still he slept with his back against my leg or stretched himself on three chairs but put his head on my lap. After some weeks he began to talk aggressively, to complain of the school, of various members of the staff and of myself in particular. With almost startling suddenness he had switched from passivity to aggression. He constantly complained that I was fat and, when I linked this with his anger at his mother's later pregnancies and his jealousy of the younger children, his aggression began to take the form of personal rivalry with the other children.
> Before real regression had taken place he had been in a suicidal frame of mind, with aggression turned against himself in dangerous and compulsive climbing. Now his aggression had a new direction. It was person to person, and there were times when various members of the staff had to hold him back from doing serious injury to other children.
> Despite one or two acts of delinquency, Tony has made an excellent recovery, has become tractable, friendly and affectionate at home and in school. His school work has improved and there is no reason to doubt that eventually he will become a good citizen.

We see here the struggle against regression and dependence upon external objects on the part of a boy who felt himself to be so rejected that to love anyone would be the ultimate risk. In every way he gave the school ample excuse to expel and reject him as he had been expelled and rejected so many times before. He volunteered to take the blame for rejection, for he could then say to himself: 'It's not that they don't love me, but my behaviour has been so bad that no one could possibly be blamed for hating me and wishing to get rid of me.' That the idea of rejection was never mooted or even hinted at gave him to hope that perhaps he had found at last an environment which really cared about him and could not be unsettled by his aggressive behaviour, and where he could also sort out the meaning of this for himself.

This hope precipitated feelings bordering on panic, and all his defences were roused to prevent himself acknowledging his longing for dependence. At this point he gave up climbing on the roof but was determined to take umbrage at every possible point. Overtly he was saying: 'I hate you all and I don't care if you do hate me.' Unconsciously he was asking himself: 'Would these people really care for me if I were to reject them instead of their rejecting me? If I were to run away and stay away, would they really accept me back?'

He had the courage to put this to the test, but before he made this desperate experiment he made sure of three things: one, by throwing a stone through my window he informed me how he felt, and that he intended to go; two, by abusing me roundly I would have every excuse for rejecting him; and three, he was using me as a 'supplementary ego' – making *me* feel the pain in the experience (to the full impact of which he was partially anæsthetized) and the stark reality of the offence. Once he had risked everything on this desperate throw, and discovered that he had been taken back into the school without question and that I had understood the need and the meaning behind the process, he was able, in one rapid move, to regress to a childlike state of complete trust and dependence and get in touch with both his depression and his longing to recapture the mood and security of the infant. It is the capacity not only to recognize the need for regression, but to understand and interpret it to the child, and meet it, that is the special role of a school such as Bredinghurst.

· · · · ·

METHOD

While only about fifty per cent. of the boys receive psychotherapy proper while they are in residence, every child benefits from the general psychiatric orientation of the school. Once each member of the staff is able to accept the psychiatric point of view and regards his task as therapeutic rather than punitive or mere charitable concern, the whole nature of the institution changes dramatically and fundamentally. The school is not thought of as a place of detention to which anti-social children are sentenced for a time or in which they are 'put-away'. It is not considered to be the duty of the school to 'bring home' to a boy the enormity of his crime or dragoon him into an understanding of the hurt he has caused his parents or the harm he has inflicted on society. To superimpose yet another burden of guilt on to an already complicated psychic pattern can only serve to militate against ultimate cure and actively prevent the child from getting in touch with his own primitive guilt feelings and his need to make restitution.

Though it is true that one of the major aims of the school is to relieve society of the incubus of the emotionally ill and delinquent child, so long as the child is in the school our concern must be with him as a patient, with *his* problem rather than society's, with his inner unconscious sense of guilt rather than legal complications, with his eventual health rather than the immediate convenience or comfort of the staff.

If one factor has contributed more than others to the remarkably high standard of success achieved at Bredinghurst in the treatment of emotional disorders it has been the awareness shown by all members of the staff of the unconscious motives and fantasies which impel a child towards actions which are socially unacceptable. We have found that the majority of workers genuinely wish to know more about the children in their charge and have enough sensibility to realize that a boy who steals may be trying to lay his hand on an inner conflict rather than outward object. They are impressed not with the badness of these boys, but with their infinite sadness; with their good intentions that get lost somewhere in the process of execution, and with their desperate need and longing for affection. In the setting of the psychiatrically orientated school it is possible to make some headway in explaining and clarifying the role of unconscious fantasy and the effect of early anxiety-situations on the development of the child, the incomplete conscience (super-ego), and the devious paths by which the child tries to arrive at personal integration.

What those who imagine that moral instruction will suffice fail to realize is that moral instruction can appeal only to the conscience of the child, and it is exactly in his conscience (super-ego) that he is most crippled either because it is adynamic and incomplete, or because he has become the victim of its overdevelopment. In either case to make an appeal to the conscience and to lofty moral principles in the early stages of treatment is like expecting a boy with no arms to put up a good fight, and shows no understanding whatever of the problem upon which we are engaged. It is important, therefore, for the psychiatric staff to be able to explain the maladjusted child's need to correct and test his unconscious fantasies against the stable reality and normality of parent surrogates, and in the therapeutic situation generally. Maladjusted and delinquent behaviour constitutes a flight from inner fantasy. To bombard the child with moral principles, to expect him to conform to external norms, to make him anxious lest his new environment will reject him through his ill-behaviour is to prevent him from getting in touch with his unconscious fantasies.

I may perhaps compress the whole problem thus:

Maladjustment can be cured only by the environment's taking a real part in the child's life.

If the environment gives him no opportunity to turn in on himself and get in touch with his unconscious fantasies, he will be overtly delinquent or anti-social.

If psychotherapy is provided, it improves the tolerance of the managing environment, and it enables the child to tolerate fantasy.

It can be categorically stated, therefore, that only when psychotherapy can be provided and matched with a truly sympathetic care-taking environment can the cure of the more disturbed child take place. A school which can accept the analytical point of view is able to contain and cure boys who, had they been at another school, would have been considered incurable, sent on to an approved school and probably have become psychopaths. Fortunately for Bredinghurst the more disturbed boys are in treatment with the therapist. This means that much less acting-out, uncontrollable behaviour, violence, and delinquency takes place than would otherwise be the case because the analyst is able to help the child discover and keep in touch with his inner fantasies and not translate repressed fantasies directly into anti-social acts.

In a later chapter we shall deal more fully with the question of discipline as it bears on the clinical aspect of treatment. Here I need only explain how discipline fits into the general running of the school and becomes an integral part of the therapeutic method. We are strongly opposed to the notion that the disturbed child can be cured or materially helped by the wholesale removal of all forms of external sanction, by the complete absence of discipline in the conventional sense. Nothing, in our experience, is better designed to cast a child into a vortex of anxiety than the haphazard relaxation of adult authority. Though many of the children who come into our care have been physically assaulted by their parents, or subjected to various vicious and cruel forms of discipline, most frequently they come from homes where there has been no steady and sustained disciplinary foundation. The parents are always individuals who are themselves inadequate in a variety of ways and who have, generally, vacillated between extreme laxity and physical brutality, between indifference and sentimental concern. These children have been caught up in and confused by the disorderly personalities of their parents, by very real mental illness in the home or by a fundamental lack of security in the family setting. To imagine that they would benefit from a carefully tailored anarchic structure within the school is no more than pseudo-psychological caprice.

This must not lead anyone to suppose that we have established a rigid régime within the school in the hope that a child will learn only that society has a very muscular arm which it has no hesitation in using against the transgressor. Yet discipline there must be. Good discipline is not monochromatic conformity. Bredinghurst has no uniform, no creed, no written code or rules, no regimentation. But any form of communal living in which each member does as he wishes ceases forthwith to be a community. There must be some basic conformity, some set standard of behaviour and expectation, otherwise the group merely provides a milieu of anarchy which prevents the disturbed child from being able to demarcate his own areas of anarchy, his own disturbance being swallowed up in a general disarray.

The sanctions at Bredinghurst are very much the same as those to be found at a boarding-school for normal children, though there is a very real recognition that at certain times it is not only impossible, but actually imperative, for a boy to disregard them and know himself to be in open or covert revolt. School hours are the same as those in a normal school and a boy is expected to work to the best of his ability. The routine of rising, meal-times, classes, and bedtime is fixed. Reasonable standards of tidiness, cleanliness, and orderly behaviour are set. Punishments may vary from loss of privileges, deprivation of pocket-money, detention, and loss of home-leave, to corporal punishment – though the latter is seldom resorted to.

At no time, however, is it lost sight of that these boys are not able always to match up to the minimum social demands which would be made upon the normal child in the conventional school, and that to enforce such demands might, in certain cases, militate against cure. Each child must be treated as an individual and each misdemeanour considered in the light of the known inner stresses which he endures. There is consequently a singular degree of tolerance shown towards each child in certain circumstances and this leniency is seldom misunderstood by the other boys. They are able to accept that justice does not necessarily demand that everyone shall at all times be treated in exactly the same way.

In the boarding-school much depends upon the provision of a setting in which there can be affectionate and sensitive management of the child on the part of the resident house-staff. The mental and emotional disturbances from which these children suffer are usually the result of false, unreal, or unhealthy relationships between themselves and their parents. Correction of the affective predicament will involve the child attaching himself to parental figures in the school, and the house-staff will thus become the objects of the child's need for love, dependence, defiance and hate. It follows that they must be capable of tolerance, forbearance, intuitive understanding and extreme resilience. They must not be unwilling to accept the parental role.

Anna Freud and Dorothy Burlingham[2] demonstrated the vital importance of the mother surrogate. They reported:

2. *Young Children in Wartime*, Allen & Unwin, London, 1942.

'The step taken was the subdivision of the large nursery group into six small "family groups" of about four children. In assigning the children to their new substitute mothers, we followed the signs of preference on the one hand by the children, and on the other hand by the young workers. Each 'mother' now has more or less complete charge of her family. She alone bathes and dresses her group, is responsible for their clothes and offers them protection against all the current mishaps of nursery life. There is no necessity any longer to refuse a child special attention of a motherly kind.

'The result of this arrangement was astonishing in its force and immediacy. The need for individual attachment for the feelings which had been lying dormant came out in a rush. In the course of one week all six families were completely and firmly established. But the reactions in the beginning were far from being exclusively happy ones. Since all these children had already undergone a painful separation from their own mothers, their mother-relationship is naturally burdened with the effects of this experience. To have a mother means, to them equally, the possibility of losing the mother; the love for the mother being thus closely accompanied by the hate and resentment produced by her supposed desertion. Consequently the violent attachment to the mother substitutes of their own choice was anything but peaceful for the children. They clung to them, full of possessiveness and anxiety when they were present, anxiously watched every one of their movements toward the door of the nursery and would burst into tears whenever they were left by them for a few minutes.

'Jealousy developed alongside the mother-attachment. There were two types of jealousy to be seen: one directed against the children of the same family group who actually shared the attention of the mother substitute; or when the children succeeded in accepting these brothers and sisters who were forced on them, they directed the full impact of their jealousy against the children outside their family group, and would not allow their worker to have any dealings with them. . . . Fights among the children multiplied in frequency and intensity.

'Luckily this state of affairs did not last longer than two or three weeks. With the realization that their new mother substitute really belonged to them, reappeared as often as she disappeared and had no intention to desert them altogether, the state of frenzy subsided and gave way to a quieter, more stable and comforting attachment. At the same time the children began to develop in leaps and bounds. The most gratifying effect was that several children who had seemed hopeless as far as the training for cleanliness was concerned suddenly started to use the pot regularly and effectively.'

This passage shows in clear definition the importance of the mother-surrogate, and the principles here elaborated are the same as those on which the cottage system succeeds with the older child. In much the same vein Stanton and Schwartz[3] discuss an article contributed to the *American Journal of Orthopsychiatry* by Bruno Bettleheim and Emmy Sylvester[4] in which they describe the syndrome of psychological institutionalism. Their comments are relevant here, for the one thing that all boys admitted to schools for maladjusted children have in common is that they are emotionally deprived, and a surprising percentage have previously spent many years in institutions.

'Bettleheim and Sylvester described a syndrome of psychological institutionalism as an emotional deficiency disease occuring in children who have been in a certain kind of institution for a period of time, or who have been shifted from one home to another: its cause they believe to be the "absence of interpersonal relationships" particularly with adults, who have become shadowy figures rather than intimate ones. Determination of his behaviour by external rules prevents the child from developing his own controls, deprives him of adequate parental images around which integration may centre, and leads to passive submission, without spontaneity or the growth of reality testing in diversified conditions of life.

'The authors go on to say that pleasure and tension were felt almost wholly in relation to the children's own bodies and were only very loosely associated with the adults responsible for their care. In contrast when these children were placed in another milieu where consistency was not primarily represented by impersonal rules by one person who supervised all of each child's activities, who personified consistency rather than enforcing or preaching it, the children showed a spontaneous growth in tolerating and then enjoying a relationship with an adult; internalization of controls appeared, along with some flexibility and spon-

3. *The Mental Hospital*. Allen and Unwin, London, 1942, p.16f.
4. 'A Therapeutic Milieu'. *American Journal of Orthopsychiatry:* Vol. 18 (1948), pp.191-206.

taneity. For these children a therapeutic milieu was a *personal* one, where questions of schedule and routine were subservient to highly individualized and spontaneous interpersonal relationships. The picture of "psychological institutionalism" as described by these authors in relation to children resembles a frequent picture of chronic schizophrenia.'

The value and importance of providing this intimate contact and supporting milieu for the disturbed child cannot easily be exaggerated. At the time of maximum need he can take for granted the strength and affection of the adult upon whom he depends. He must feel secure enough to be hostile and to express anxiety about his feelings of dependence, so that he can do so without despair, or guilt, or shame, knowing that the mature staff-member expects violent mood swings and, unlike his own parents, does not interpret hatred and hostility as a final breakdown in the relationship. The aim of the cottage-staff must always be to offer love, without themselves becoming so involved in the child's life as to feel deprived and excessively anxious when negative feelings are in the ascendent. There is no room for patronage or condescension. The children are not here to be done good to. They are developing, growing organisms in a living association with real people who are sufficiently detached not to be thrown into emotional panic by eccentric behaviour on the part of the child.

It is recognized that a child will show marked preference for one or other of the staff. It follows from this that the adults must hold themselves available to the child at all reasonable times. Time and inclination must allow for real companionship in order that the boy may be able to feel his way into a relationship with an adult who, while kindly and sympathetic, has a full and rounded existence apart from the child. Despite the close attachments made within the school there is no intention whatever of undermining the child's relationship with his real parents. Eventually, if all goes well, he will return to his family and be able to resume his place in the home, but now able to make a positive attachment and contribution to the very environment in which he first became disturbed.

This can seldom be achieved rapidly. There is no magic in therapy. It is a conscious technique in which one works within a known framework and keeps in harmony with the varying phases of development in the child. One of the chief criticisms of our work is that it takes time, generally a long time. But when it is seen not as a health-cure but as a long and complicated process of regression, co-ordination and growth, it is obvious that speed is impossible. The average length of stay for a boy at Bredinghurst is about three years. A few boys have been discharged within a year; others have been in residence and under treatment for as long as seven years.

Parents usually find some difficulty in accustoming themselves to the notion that their children will be away from home for so long a time. They find it hard to accept that their child is so ill that prolonged treatment is necessary. They often hope that we shall teach the boy a short, sharp lesson, and that the pain of separation will quickly 'bring him to his senses'. Many a mother has used her child as a convenient external vehicle for her own depression, hatred, or fears of gross emotional disturbance. Consequently when the boy is away from home she is thrust back upon her own illness and may become quickly depressed or disorganized, or her hatred may be transferred to another child or her husband. Such parents are for ever pleading with us to let their child return home. They are quickly convinced that he is 'better', that we have rapidly achieved a remarkable change in the boy and it is time they had him back. Some obvious behavioural difficulty in the child, bed-wetting or stealing, may have been the one symptom upon which the parents have concentrated their attention and, once this symptom has cleared up, it is not always easy for them to accept that there is any justification in our continuing to regard the child as ill and in need of further treatment.

Occasionally parental anxieties are so acute that a child will be removed from our care despite our best endeavours to persuade the parents against such a course. If the boy is not on a Fit Person Order the parents are legally at liberty to take him home. On several occasions this has happened, only for us to receive frantic appeals to re-admit the boy a few weeks later.

> In the first week James, a lad of thirteen, ran back home three times, but during the second week he showed signs of settling down. At his interview with the psychiatrist it was discovered that he slept in the same bed as his mother and mutual sexual fondling took place. The father slept in a separate bedroom.

The fact that the boy showed some slight sign of being able to exist apart from his mother immediately threw her into a panic, and at the end of the second week she arrived at the school with a large suit-case, determined to take her boy back. She was dissuaded.

James had several sessions with the psychotherapist and, though withdrawn and sullen, was able to say that he found some relief in being away from a cramping home situation. When he went home for a week-end he told his mother that he was reasonably contented at the school and had made friends with another boy. At the begining of the next week his mother appeared again with her suit-case and, despite all we could do, removed the child. Several years later we learned that he was in an approved school.

In the main, however, parents come to recognize that their child is ill and are not unwilling for treatment to continue for as long as we deem it necessary.

Once a boy has begun to make obvious improvement the parents usually tell the social worker that they have been considering having the child home and ask her opinion. She attempts to discover whether they and the child have gained a real measure of tolerance and mutual understanding. This can often be judged to some extent by the feeling in the home when the boy has been with the family for one of the long holidays. The boy, too, will have broached the subject with the therapist or the headmaster and the possibility of discharge is then discussed in conference. If it is agreed by all the staff that the child has reached a stage where he can be returned home and can also attend an ordinary day-school he is normally discharged at the end of the current term.

For a variety of reasons not all the children discharged are able to go home. In such cases they may be transferred to another residential school, to foster-parents or, if of school-leaving age, to a hostel.

We endeavour to keep in touch for an indefinite period with every boy who has been through Bredinghurst, but this has its complications. Some parents do not welcome continued contact with the school and some boys do not wish to be reminded that at one time they were 'deemed maladjusted'.

This sentiment we respect and the social worker does not keep in touch directly with the family if they express the wish, or she senses it, not to be reminded of the past. But even in such instances we get information through other social agencies, so that we can in almost every case tell exactly what has happened to any boy after he has left us.

The great majority of the boys keep in touch with the school on their own accord. They are free to visit us at any time and, if they wish, to stay for a meal or a week-end. Many of them write from time to time to members of the staff for whom they have formed a particular attachment. For a large number of these boys Bredinghurst has become very much a second home and, in some cases, the only home they have ever known. It is not surprising, therefore, that they should wish to keep us informed of their careers and circumstances long after they have ceased to be members of the school.

4

The Maladjusted Child

To define a condition adds little to the understanding of it, but it does at least outline the framework in which understanding may be achieved. Many attempts have been made to define 'maladjustment', but none is completely satisfactory. In one sense the whole of this book is little more than an attempt at a definition; for what maladjustment may mean is inherent in the case material and varies both in nature and intensity from one case to another.

On the broadest canvas what we envisage by maladjustment is no more nor less than the fact that a child is unable to live healthily in the normal context of home or school without pain to himself or disturbance to his environment. It is, of course, possible for a child in certain circumstances to live without obvious personal distress or overt delinquency in a severely ill and oppressive home. But here our emphasis would be on the word 'healthily' in our tentative definition. The overt signs of emotional disturbance might be delayed till much later in life and be projected on to a complicated adult situation or assimilated into a distorted character structure or other forms of affective disturbance which, though not openly in conflict with the social environment, can have very invidious effects within the inter-personal relations of such an individual or his family life, thus perpetuating a problem socially.

The treatment of the problem of maladjustment implies, therefore, not solely the resolution of obvious anti-social behaviour or character defects, but, as importantly, the ability to detect, rightly diagnose and treat emotional illness in the child who has not acquired a reputation for delinquency nor attracted attention to himself as an obviously disturbed individual. Thus a school for maladjusted children, though it must inevitably house and handle delinquent children, does more than attempt to promote health in the child who is a social menace. It is, first and foremost, concerned with the individual as a problem to, and within, himself whether or not this problem is reflected in anti-social behaviour. Once it can be accepted that maladjustment is a mute appeal for new understanding, the child's attempt to focus attention upon a predicament he can sense but not verbalize, it is possible to ask what is the 'meaning' of maladjustment.

Aichhorn[1] and Healy and Bronner,[2] among others, have suggested that the hidden significance of anti-social behaviour deserves close examination. Delinquency, they claim, may be a compensatory satisfaction, an attempt to bolster up an inadequate ego through the local prestige of notoriety, a revenge attitude, a form of seeking punishment to allay deep and unconscious feelings of guilt, and so on. This we do not doubt. Our contention is, however, that the child cannot profitably explore nor begin to verbalize his feelings unless he can first be provided with a secure emotional milieu. Lacking this, he can only attain a halfway-house on the road to health. This may be some advantage to him and lead to the elimination or diminution of some of his symptoms but must not be mistaken for recovery. An interesting statement by Dr D. W. Winnicott on this aspect of the problem is to be found in his *Collected Papers*[3] where he relates it to the establishment of a 'false self' in the psychoses: 'Where there is a high degree of the tendency to a split at this early stage,' he writes, 'the individual is in danger of being seduced into a false life, and the instincts then come in on the side of the seducing environment. Pediatrics at its worst (i.e. accent on physical health, denial of psyche-claims) can be said to be the organized exploitation of the betrayal of human nature by the instincts. A successful seduction of this kind may produce a false self that seems satisfactory to the unwary observer, although the schizophrenia is latent and will claim attention in the end. The false self developed on a compliance basis cannot attain to the independence of maturity, except perhaps a psuedo-maturity in a psychotic environment.'

It is exactly this 'pseudo-maturity' in a false environment that is the snare in which so many good intentions in the treatment of maladjusted children get caught. A high percentage of children

1. *Wayward Youth*. Putnam, London, 1936. p.37f.
2. *New Light on Delinquency*. Yale, New Haven, 1936, p.133f.
3. Tavistock, London, 1958, p.225.

are discharged from schools as fit to return home, and deemed no longer maladjusted, because their behaviour over a considerable period in the school has been exemplary and they appear to have made a good adaptation to life. But once these children return to a normal environment and the ordinary family setting they rapidly break down or show in their further development that residential treatment without psychotherapy had, in fact, arrested them somewhere short of true health. We may, perhaps, go so far as to say that only in the kind of setting which a school like Bredinghurst can provide and which includes psychotherapy can the child feel safe enough, and understood enough, to be able to reveal the true nature and extent of his illness. In this sense, then, the first obligation of the school might be said to be to let the child become as ill as he really is, to slough off his defences and false adjustments to a false environment.

Many of the parents of the boys in Bredinghurst complain, after their child has been in residence some few months, that 'he appears to be getting worse'. That this happens in the majority of cases is, in our view, a sign that the initial task of the school is being achieved, for the child feels himself to be in an environment sufficiently understanding and secure for him to be able to let go his defences and make little or no attempt to disguise his disturbance. We would claim, then, that the paramount appeal of maladjustment in the child is for a new setting and new framework of relationships in which he may gain security, release, insight, self-respect, and finally self-control – in that order. To imagine that strict adult control will lead by a short route to self-control is to fail to understand the intricate nature of the task.

It has been our experience that the boys at the school become by degrees more deeply aware of their predicament, of the nature of their illness and the fragility of their ego-development than they would have been (or been able to convey) had they remained in the normal home setting – and this even in cases where psychotherapy is not available to them. This must in large part explain why it is that though the majority of our patients have been in treatment at Child Guidance Clinics they have not been able to explore to any depth the painfully sensitive, confused, and unformed areas of their personalities.

As already mentioned some educationists find it impossible to equate delinquency and unmanageable behaviour with illness in any guise. To them, anti-social behaviour is no more than deliberate wrong-headedness, a churlish revolt against society. The weakness of this position is exposed when it is observed that these are the people who are most easily persuaded to change their mental attitude, though not their unconscious bias, towards the delinquent by an appeal to sentimentality. It would be a simple matter in work of this kind to drag up a spurious kind of sympathy for the maladjusted child by briefly sketching in the tragic and turbulent backgrounds of some of the boys who have been under treatment with us, by tracing word-pictures of the mad, unreal, violent, or indifferent homes in which they have been brought up. But sentimentality has no place whatever in therapy.

Nevertheless, some appreciation of the internal world in which the child lives is of value. It is not in any great measure different from the graphic description given by Stanton and Schwartz[4] of the adult mental patient:

'To describe the role of the mental patient in the formal sense . . . is to run the risk of minimising the vast amount of suffering the mental patient experiences, and to overlook the indefiniteness, complexity and subtlety involved in "being a mental patient". It is hard to keep in mind what it means subjectively to be a mental patient; to be so fearful that each aspect of the environment represents a threat to one's existence; to experience the world as unreal and to see the "outside" as just a flimsy structure with no substance; to live with the feeling of restraint and being closed in, or suffocated, and to feel rebellion and resentment at this and be unable to express it in any effective way; to experience utter, desperate, and unrelieved loneliness, with no hope of change; to feel that in the entire universe there is no person that will ever understand one; to believe that one's actions have no effect and that one is not affected by the actions of others. To be a mental patient means to feel removed from the human race and to view oneself as not quite human; it means the inability to think or to trust one's thoughts; it means to be lacking in privacy and to be exposed to the view of strangers, when association with everyone is a thing to be dreaded and shunned. For association with others is unpredictable; it may be terrible in many different ways; one may be treated with contempt or one may experience the delicious surprise of being treated very

4. *The Mental Hospital*, p.194ff.

gently, and this may be even worse for it arouses hope, and hope always means some internal upheaval. The world of the mental patient is a world of anxiety.'

In maladjusted children, by comparison, there is a relative lack of structure, the child not yet having opted finally for a completely ill and unreal inward mental construction. This is probably the reason why, if admitted and treated while still comparatively young, they yield better therapeutic results than when they are admitted towards the close of their school careers. By the time a boy reaches the age of thirteen, or thereabouts, his reaction-formations become statically embedded in character-traits of defiance and violence. In order to deal with so set a condition more intensive treatment over a longer period is necessary and this the school may not be in a position to offer.

Whether or not a boy has been told the nature of the school in which he finds himself, he has a shrewd idea of its function and of the condition in himself which has led to his being there. Some boys have been told by their parents that they are merely 'going to a boarding-school because you are backward in education'. Others have long been warned that if their behaviour does not improve they will be 'sent away' and, on the surface, accept that their arrival at the school is no more than the fulfilment of a threat. Yet behind this mask of acceptance on the parents' pragmatic level is always a deeper understanding of the significance of what has taken place. Occasionally a boy can say in the first interview how relieved he is to have escaped from a painful home situation, or, denying his anxiety and exposing his feelings of omnipotence, declare: 'I always wanted to come here and at last my parents have agreed.' To a remarkable degree the ill child can assess the seriousness of his predicament, find comfort in the undenied statement that this is a school for 'boys who are ill', and make allowances for the odd and outlandish behaviour, mannerisms, and grimaces of the other children.

One of the unfortunate consequences of the pitifully inadequate provision of psychotherapy for children in our society is that only a percentage of the boys at Bredinghurst can receive sustained treatment. Invariably there are more boys in the school who we feel could benefit from psychotherapy than there is time in which to treat them. I am always being pressed by one boy or another to include him in my schedule. The only compromise in such cases is to see the child occasionally, at times of maximum need or stress. But the fact that this kind of appeal is made almost every day shows clearly that these boys are aware of the purpose of therapy and of their own internal disorganization. In a few cases it has been the importunity of a boy who had previously not been scheduled for treatment that has persuaded me to accept him as a patient. It is not that we regard such a boy as being his own diagnostician, but that, as in normal society, the voluntary patient is acknowledging his need and his sense of urgency combined with hope.

There is a pathetic quality about the comfort which so many of the boys find in the open acceptance of their illness, as in the boy who told me with a real sense of relief: 'We are all mad here,' and in his obvious gratitude for my refusal to deny his assessment of the situation. He had long been the only member in a seriously deranged home who had been sufficiently sane to acknowledge his own mental and emotional instability.

Sensitivity to one's own inner dilemma may open floodgates of compassion to the predicaments of others. For this reason there is a surprisingly high level of relatively normal community living at Bredinghurst. Meaningful friendships are formed, quite astonishing tolerance is shown towards bizarre behaviour in some of the boys, and the children use one another in acting-out their personal problems and tensions. This has its benign aspects, as when a boy says to me: 'You really ought to see Peter, you know. He's as nutty as a fruit-cake.' Here the child is not only admitting his own fear of madness, but is showing a genuine regard for the needs and right of others. Another patient said: 'I think that new boy ought to be on your list. He had a fit last night and then was crying in bed for hours and banging his head against the wall. He's just the sort of case for you. I couldn't help feeling sorry for the poor little bastard.'

Incidents of this kind, and the capacity of boys who are feeling more at ease to make some direct contribution to the emotional needs of both child and adult members of the school, illustrate the element of constructive restitution and reparation[5] which is so essential a process in the struggle towards emotional health. Restitutive activities, in a healthy and positive dimension, become possible within the school setting in contrast to the helplessness of making any such gestures in the home setting.

5. See Winnicott, D. W., op.cit. xii, xviii, xxi.

Sometimes these gestures are touchingly delicate and generous. One boy, for example, who had gone through a particularly violent and destructive phase culminating in an appearance in court, where I had pleaded for him, spent his next session with me in a long discussion on legal procedure. He had been impressed with the obvious kindliness of the woman magistrate before whom he had appeared, and with the eminently fair and human manner in which the detective had presented the case. He had also been genuinely distressed by the sight of so many other children waiting for their cases to be heard, and told me how sorry he felt for them in that they did not have Bredinghurst behind them. In fact he thought that it must be a wonderful thing to be a barrister and try to find ways of helping delinquents who could not help themselves, and wished that he had the intelligence and opportunity to become one himself. Before he left he pressed into my hand a small parcel, tied with blue ribbon, and, with obvious excitement, asked me to open it. Inside was a small bar of chocolate.

I knew that to buy this he must have used virtually all his pocket-money, and that he also had to save up to pay his fine. But he would not hear of my even sharing the chocolate with him. That I was obviously moved and appreciative was his reward. 'But,' I said, 'you must have used all your pocket-money to get me this.' 'That's all right,' he replied with a casual gesture of the hand, 'I'll be getting ninepence next Saturday. Besides I've got a half-penny left.'

Less benign is the prevalence of bullying in a school where sadistic and masochistic personality formations find in one another ample opportunity for mutual exploitation. Much bullying is the inevitable consequence of rivalry and jealousy between siblings and the very frequency with which it occurs is, in an odd way, a tribute to the success of the school in that it reflects the deep attachments and transference feelings from the boys towards various members of the staff:

> Keith, who had been in treatment for about ten months and who, till now, had been able to talk freely, suddenly became quiet and remote during his hours with me. He would sit and look out of the window, or play aimlessly with wooden blocks on the floor. Any comment of mine was greeted with an outburst of swearing or else I was merely commanded peremptorily to 'shut up, you dirty cunt!'

During this week I had been getting constant reports from the house and teaching staff that Keith was bullying the smaller boys viciously – a thing he had not done before.

I noted, however, that while playing he would ask several times during the session: 'Are you fat, Doc?' As soon as he had asked the question he would make loud noises which seemed to me to be designed to prevent his hearing whatever reply I might make. If I raised my voice he would increase his noises, in an attempt to drown my words. Eventually I shouted above the din: 'No, Keith, I'm not pregnant!' At this he suddenly leapt up and began to hit me repeatedly in the stomach, yelling: 'You fucking well are, you stinking bastard!' When he had calmed himself somewhat I was able to relate his questions about my fatness, his bullying of smaller boys, and his sudden anger with me to his own feelings of anxiety, fear and hatred at the time of the birth of his younger brother. In fact, Keith's inability to bear rivalry with other children in the home for his mother's love had led him, a few months earlier, to assist his twin brother in trying to commit suicide. The twin had decided to take an overdose of aspirin and Keith had helped him find sufficient tablets and had encouraged him to eat them.

At the close of this session he was able to tell me how deeply he resented my treating anyone other than him in the school and how much he resented my having children of my own.

Instances of this kind could be recounted by virtually every member of the staff. They underline the importance of having workers who can understand that outbursts of apparently irrational behaviour are not merely due to some perverse factor in the child's character, but have a cogency of their own. The transference situation with its concomitant recrudescence of infantile feelings has a substantive logic in the unconscious. Temper tantrums and outbursts of violent behaviour are easily tolerated in the small child of three or four. But when the same intensity of feeling is expressed by a boy just short of fifteen, with a strong frame and near-adult musculature, it is sometimes difficult to sympathize or contend with them. In fact the disparity between the intensity of childhood emotions released and the age and physical strength of the patient is one of the principle problems facing the staff in an institution of this kind, for some of the staff tend to expect standards of behaviour and control that correspond with the child's chronological age.

If treatment of the maladjusted child is to be successful it is incumbent on the staff if they cannot understand the hidden logic in the child's bizarre behaviour at least to tolerate it, acknowledging that the boy is compelled by inner forces to act on a plane and from motives which are not related to his present situation except in so far as he draws unconscious parallels between his present setting and that which characterized his infancy. Educationally, intellectually, and physically he lives in the present: emotionally he lives in the past.

The aim of psychotherapy in a school environment is to help the child gain sufficient insight into himself and his motives as to be able to bring forward repressed emotions, test them against reality, and so realign his affective life with his true age and present setting. To achieve these ends inevitably means that the child has to break down defensive inward structures that have served him in the past, and this is productive of great anxiety in himself. It places, for a time, a heavy burden of responsibility on the therapeutic environment which has to hold him over a period of partial disintegration before true emotional integration can take place.

From the point of view of the convenience of the administration and management it is infinitely less wearing on the staff if they choose to rely upon the traditional admixture of charity, moral instruction, and rigid discipline. Such a technique emphasizes the present and attempts to persuade the patient to adjust himself to the world as he finds it. It encourages the disturbed boy to 'act his age', to assume responsibilities consistent with his physical growth, and to conform to adult standards of morals and behaviour. This ignores altogether the fact that he cannot avoid living in the past. It disregards completely the chronological dichotomy which is inherent in the emotional indisposition of the child.

It is, of course, a gross oversimplification to say that the purpose of a school such as Bredinghurst is to create a situation in which infantile logic is accepted as the basis of understanding. But unless an attempt is made to do this there can be no hope of ultimate cure, only of a superimposed discipline which may break down completely when the child leaves the protected atmosphere, and which does nothing to set right the basic failure in interpersonal relationships.

To school a child into a fear of the law to such a degree that he is never again delinquent may be a very real advantage to society, but it does little or nothing to ensure the patient's capacity to lead a full life, to make wholesome attachments in marriage, or to make use of his latent personal qualities. In addition it may be pointed out that merely to inculcate a discipline that will prevent further delinquency is not necessarily to relieve society of an incubus, for delinquency suppressed but uncured in this generation is very prone to appear in the next. Such an individual, while renouncing delinquency for himself, is most likely to create a home situation for his children in which they become the avenue for his unfulfilled delinquent proclivities.

We return, therefore, to the position which we took up at the outset of this chapter: namely, that the purpose of the school is not simply to find a path by which the disturbed child can be less of a burden to his social environment, but to provide a setting and adequate treatment in which he can match up his internal logic with the outside world and, in so doing, free that part of his personality which has been engrossed in the past, and thereby grasp health for himself and live in harmony with society.

5

Discipline

THERE are two diametrically opposed points of view about discipline in schools for maladjusted children, with neither of which do we agree. There are those who believe that the best kind of environment for disturbed children is one in which there is virtually no imposed discipline whatever.[1] The child is given complete freedom to do as he wishes, to attend classes when he pleases, get up and go to bed when he chooses, and generally organize his life according to his own whim. This policy is based on the assumption that every child possesses a native, internal, structural health, a capacity for self-discipline of a socially acceptable variety, which needs only a permissive environment for it to become apparent. The opposite view is taken by those who contend that if the child is compelled by severe sanctions to conform to a rigid code of moral and social behaviour while at school, he will in time become so accustomed to thinking and acting in this way that he will conform automatically thereafter because he has discovered from experience that the penalties for disobedience are too harsh to be risked.

Both of these points of view fail to take into account the psychology of the maladjusted and delinquent child, or, indeed, of the normal child. I would define our position in the following way:

(a) It is necessary to bear in mind that there is an inherent conflictual element in normal human development. Not only are there unconscious conflicts for the child on the way towards individuality, but there is also the fact of tension between himself and his environment which helps him to feel whole, a separate person. If he is placed in an environment which refuses to

---

1. Cp. Neil, A. S. *The Problem Child.* Jenkins, London, 1929; also Burn, M. *Mr Lyward's Answer.* Hamish Hamilton, London, 1956.

recognize the existence of any conflict whatever and merely encourages him to do as he wishes, he is made to feel anxious and unreal. The external world has become as unformed and lacking in structure as his inner world, thus giving him no sense of being 'held' or cared for. He interprets lack of discipline as lack of interest and, consequently, feels vaguely hostile towards the permissive environment.

(b) All maladjusted and delinquent children have already achieved dynamic distortions which need active therapeutic undoing and resolution. If maladjustment were merely a question of immaturity in ego-development, it might be logical to assume that given wise environmental handling recovery would spontaneously occur. Such a construction, however, totally ignores the fact that in all delinquents there has taken place an active distortion of the personality which needs correction, which needs to be set against healthier modes of affectivity and thought, and which demands considerable insight on the part of the patient if health is to be established. Without psychotherapy the child is unable to examine the false premises upon which he has built up false and anti-social behaviour patterns.

(c) The delinquent's dependence on his maladjustment through anxiety is also a factor which needs active therapeutic procedures rather than mere permissiveness. Here the delinquent's proclivity to take paths of least resistance and exploit leniency in adults is of importance. Most maladjusted children interpret leniency beyond a certain point as weakness, lack of interest, veiled hostility, or abject fear.

(d) Neither the advocates of the permissive environment nor those who advocate harsh discipline take into account the unconscious defence mechanisms in the maladjusted child. Neither technique has any instrument by which the adult can get behind the observed behaviour of the child and interpret to him the hidden motives and defences which prevent him from arriving at complete maturity and affective normalcy.

(e) It has also to be borne in mind that the delinquent takes flight from reality to a pleasure-principle magic world. There is an extreme dissociation between the areas where he suffers pain and anxiety and those in which he compensates himself by flight and magical gestures of relief. The fact that the disturbed home setting and œdipal[2] relationships have not let these children work through primitive emotional conflicts, inherent in human development, has pushed them to precocious defensive attitudes. They thus present a complicated clinical problem which needs active therapeutic measures if it is to be resolved – not mere goodwill on the part of the new environment.

The child's capacity to find socially acceptable forms of behaviour, and to arrive at some measure of self-discipline, depends very largely upon the ability of the school to provide a secure setting. Within this given structure the child is able freely to test out the limits of his strength, the tolerance of the environment, and his own need to identify himself with standards of conduct which permit a maximum degree of interchange and understanding between himself and those around him. Perhaps the primary need of the small child, viewed in this aspect, is that of knowing that his maximum strength is not able to disturb or destroy the environment upon which he depends for his own security. In small children outbursts of rage can easily be contained by the parents. A boy of five or six in a temper tantrum may throw himself in fury upon his mother, and kick and scream and become completely possessed with rage. Yet he is reassured to discover when the storm has passed that no damage has been done. His mother is still a whole person, in command of the situation, and has neither yielded her position nor suffered any physical hurt.

In this manner a child finds from experience that the most aggressive and destructive elements in his nature can be tolerated, that they have done nothing to destroy the social link which exists between himself and the adults upon whom he depends. It is possible for him, therefore, to feel at home in his aggressive moods and he has no need to build up inner defences against aggressive action which serve only to cripple and confine the personality. Here the valuable thing for the child is the discovery of personal hate and aggression. By getting in touch with this element in his make-up, while held securely in a loving relationship, he learns how to curb his anger through love of the mother.

Within the school setting this is very often the climax of treat-

2. The boy's unconscious erotic desire to possess the mother, and his consequent hostility to his father and wish to eliminate him as a rival for the mother's affections.

ment, but the climax can be reached only if there is an environment which is strong as well as loving. *If the school provides the discipline, then the therapist can provide the insight and acceptance of it. This combination of functions alone makes for the total therapeutic effect.*

The maladjusted child invariably has been unable to achieve the fusion of love and hate which the normal child achieves during his pre-school era. The mother of the delinquent child may have been obviously frightened by the intensity of infantile rage in her child and yielded to him. This then faces the infant not only with the burden of self-control at a time when he has the right to expect environmental control, but also weighs him down with a sense of guilt. The over-permissive school environment merely perpetuates this predicament, leaving the child afraid that any aggressive action on his part will lead to unreal situations and threaten an already precarious security.

The same is true of the child who has been nurtured by a mother who is physically frail or neurotically fragile or who, for any reason, is incapable of tolerating aggressive behaviour in her children. In consequence the child becomes fearful of the aggressive components in his nature and may find it necessary to cloak his emotions to an unusual degree, to deny his capacity for anger, or to find diffuse and indirect methods of dissipating aggression over a wide area of life.

In the normal home the child is able to experience anger within the context of love, and to experiment in this situation in such a way as to discover for himself that love and hate flow in parallel channels and are not diametrically opposed drives or mutually destructive, and that their interplay can enrich his inner life and experience. From this follows our contention that in the treatment of the disturbed child it is of vital importance that the school should be able to provide both firmness and affection, discipline as well as tolerance. The major problem which the school has to deal with is that by the time a child has been deemed maladjusted and placed in a residential school, he is no longer a small infant with limited strength and, consequently, little capacity for actual destructiveness, but a child who is still capable of blind fury but armed with near-adult physique. He also lacks, at the outset at least, normal sensitivity to pain in others which gives his behaviour that quality of ruthlessness which so many adults find terrifying.

The problem the school staff are faced with is that of creating an atmosphere of firm tolerance which recognizes the value of aggressive drives while at the same time having sufficient courage to be able to hold the individual child over a period of aggressive behaviour. The staff have to prevent undue damage to persons or property, take back into the school those children who have found their way to court, learn how to reply to aggression only by firmness, and, in an endless variety of ways and situations, continue to make their affection for the child real to him.

It is, of course, a measure of the child's trust in the school and of his hopes for personal recovery that he can permit himself to become aggressive, but he takes it as a matter of course that the school staff will attempt to control him when in a rage and shield others from hurt, because wild destructive rages always end in despair and hopelessness. At this point the therapist, acting as a 'supplementary ego'[3], provides the vehicle through which a meaningful psychic assimilation takes places in the child.

Ian, aged twelve, was admitted to Bredinghurst from the children's ward of a hospital for mental and nervous diseases. He was an extremely withdrawn child, his whole stance and gait conveying an air of helplessness and depression. He made no friends, did not engage in conversation, made no attempt to establish links with other boys or staff, and, in school, would sit huddled in his chair with his chin on his chest, a picture of absolute dejection. His parents had great ambitions for Ian who had succeeded in getting a place in a grammar school, but had broken down almost completely after the first term. He had a high intelligence in the region of 130. His mother was a very paranoid and confused person, affectionate but depressive and unstable. The father was a van-driver who hoped that his children would achieve what he had failed to achieve – professional status. In the home, the highest possible standards of behaviour had always been demanded, and the boy was amenable and quiet when at home.

After some months at Bredinghurst, he began in an unobtrusive manner to tease other boys, with the result that he was bullied. In a very short space of time two sides of his character could be clearly discerned; the boy seen in each phase bore no resemblance whatever to the other. For most of the day Ian would be the

3. See Heimann, P. *International Journal of Psycho-analysis*, 'On Counter-transference. (1950), Vol. xxxi and 'Dynamics of Transference Interpretation', ibid (1956), xxxviii.

depressed, shuffling, slouching, quiet figure to which we had become accustomed, but from time to time, having incited some other boy to bully him, he would become a wild raging figure intent on violence. These rages would occur with dramatic suddenness, almost as though at the flick of a switch. During these outbursts he would seize any object, a bottle, an iron bar, a cut-throat razor, and chase after his tormentor apparently bent on murder. At these times it was imperative that the staff should take some action in order to prevent grievous bodily harm.

On one occasion Ian had armed himself with an iron furnace-poker, four feet long, and began laying about him in the cottage. All the boys fled, so he smashed several panels of a cupboard and a number of banisters, and then ran out into the playground. Here he struck out at anyone who came near him. One or two members of the staff tried to persuade him to drop the poker but he refused and, whenever they came near, he would threaten them.

I came into the playground to find Ian standing in a threatening attitude with the poker above his head, and at the same time sobbing loudly. I walked with my head slightly bent as though unaware that he was armed and when I got close enough said: 'Whatever you do, Ian, don't drop that thing.' He made a gesture as though to strike me, and then held the poker above my head, his body poised to hit me with it if I made the slightest move to disarm him.

In a matter-of-fact voice I suggested that he should come over to my room and tell me all about it. I assured him that I had no intention of taking his weapon from him. This reassured him and he walked a pace or two behind me, still sobbing loudly and still holding the poker above my head, over to my room. Once there he asked me to lock the door, which I did. He sat at the desk holding the poker with both hands and indicated that I was to sit at least a yard away from him. For twenty minutes he sobbed brokenheartedly, finally laying the poker on the desk, crossing his arms over it and cradling his head in his arms.

Between fresh outbursts of sobbing we discussed the incidents that had led up to this crisis and I told him that I had not tried to take the poker from him because I realized it was vitally important to him, and did not, therefore, feel threatened by it. Gradually he became calmer and seemed to be waking from a nightmare. At the end of the hour he was able to talk rationally without undue signs of distress and as he went out left the poker standing in a corner, asking me to return it to the boiler-room.

In the course of that hour it was possible for me to watch this boy wake up from a maniacal state of rage to a gradual appreciation of the actual situation. It was possible to sit and talk with him while he, in one hour, associated these two different sides of his personality into one episode. To have taken his weapon from him, as one could have done, would not only have been to risk physical hurt, but it would also have prevented the episode from becoming a creative one for this boy and would merely have made him feel he had been assaulted. It was critically important for him to find the emotional meaning behind his wildness and thus integrate the experience into a significant communication.

For that hour the poker became for him the embodiment of his own aggression and liveliness. To have wrested it from him would have been tantamount to castration, for the poker represented for him the possession of his penis.[4] This phallic awareness, tolerated by the therapist, enabled him to feel himself to be alive, real, libidinally in contact with the outside world. He was comforted, too, by my confidence in my own strength and that I did not feel any need to end my anxiety by disarming him, that I did not feel threatened. It was enormously valuable for him to come back to a more normal frame of mind, still holding in his hand the offensive weapon and discover that no one had, in fact, been injured.

Here the therapist is acting as a supplementary ego. The boy's aliveness had suddenly overwhelmed his ego, and all he could do was maniacally express it in an outburst of destructive rage. The therapist, by introducing the element of confident acceptance of the weapon, provided an experiential link of vital importance. By saying: 'Whatever you do, don't drop that thing,' I indicated that I knew that for the time being the poker was of vital importance to him, a part of his own person, the embodiment of his liveliness. To have disarmed him would only have been to reinforce his castration anxieties and rob him of any possibility of a positive gain from the experience.

From that time on Ian gradually became a more lively child, developed an engaging sense of humour, was able to make real contacts with staff and boys, take part in games, and generally act

4. cf. Freud, Anna, *Searchlights on Delinquency*, p.193ff.

in a more gainly and spontaneous manner. Although there were many other outbursts of rage following this episode there was always now an element of conscious acting about them which made them less intense and less dangerous.

Some of the aggressive wildness of these boys is the result of primitive dissociations of affective states, where precocious defences of the ego (and of the environment) have militated against fusion of libidinal and aggressive instincts and affects. It is clear that, had the staff permitted Ian endless licence to smash and destroy property and, possibly, injure other boys, had we allowed him no contact with an adult, his whole perception of what was taking place would have been baulked. He would, in the first place, have been convinced that his feelings were too violent for the environment to cope with or resist, and he would, in consequence, have felt both guilty and frightened. Furthermore, the maniacal attack would only have led on to further 'outbursts in a vacuum' and have done nothing to establish any kind of relationship between himself and the adult world.

It is important, too, to note that some of this aggressive attack on the environment is a symbolic way of showing the total incapacity of the child's ego to master and control his inner drives. Too often the pseudo-strength of the delinquent's defiance is a cover for this inner weakness. It is exactly at this point that the child needs to rely upon the unafraid strength of the tolerant and affectionate adult to help him not only to gain insight into his own motives and anxieties, but also to experience the fact that his hope in the environment's capacity to hold him through the rageful episode was not misplaced.

One of the essential features in the treatment of maladjusted children is that once they reach a point of hope about their environment they will set out to test its strength, resilience, and sincerity. Inevitably really creative work will at some point lead to a clash between the child and the adult. The adult must expect this, be prepared for it, and not seek to take flight from personal encounter by the imposition of rigid discipline – nor by avoidance and denial which is so typical of the sentimentalist. Unaware of the need for the recognition of aggression, some teachers insist on interpreting a clash of this kind as wilful disobedience and nascent revolution. The lively aggressive anti-social child may quickly find himself classified as a 'hard case' and be threatened with immediate removal to an approved school. Such a threat in this setting is rightly understood by the child as rejection and it undercuts completely his trust in his environment and his sense of security. The child is faced with despair in a situation which had given him cause to hope. Years of good work may be nullified since the child's aliveness is felt as a threat to the school. He becomes aware that there is a low threshold of tolerance of anxiety on the part of the staff; he will conform as best he can and stubbornly refuse to get better.

The adult who has recourse to threats undermines all truly therapeutic efforts, both his own and those of other members of the staff, since he makes it obvious to the child that he can expect no adequate support from an environment which answers hopeful aggression by censure and rejection. But perhaps the least fruitful approach of all is that of the sentimentalist who appears to believe that given sufficient love and tender handling it will be possible to avoid all tension between child and adult.

From time to time individuals have worked at Bredinghurst who have gone to extraordinary lengths, when a testing situation is obviously building up in a child, to circumvent the actual climax by withdrawal, or by a grand gesture of affection, or by some weak escape into self-conscious *bonhomie*. This type of reaction has a devastating effect on the child because the picture suddenly becomes confused by the adult's anxiety thinly disguised as affection, and the whole episode peters out into meaningless futility. The child needs to be able to sense the adult's strength, his capacity to use aggression and even hatred constructively. The sentimentalist always finds work with maladjusted children a devastating and disillusioning experience. His best efforts are doomed from the start. He is forced eventually to accept that sentimentality leads to increased anxiety and bitterness in the child, and to delinquency.

Another unrewarding attitude which we have encountered is the moralistic one. A few people find their way into work with disturbed children who are convinced that the delinquent child is open to reason and can absorb and benefit from endless moral instruction. It has been our experience that these individuals invariably oscillate between high-sounding principles and total rejection of the child who does not respond to them. Children easily detect insincerity and hypocrisy, and react to it with scorn. They are aware that moralistic attitudes frequently disguise a basic lack of humanity. The type of teacher or headmaster who keeps his personal contacts with the children to a minimum but never fails to conduct morning and evening prayers and say grace before and after meals usually has a facile command of moral *bon mots* and exhortations but never becomes a real person. The 'Holy Joe' moralist is invariably capable of verbal sadism and cold dispassionate rejection; he relies on rules and regulations rather than emotional rapport, and is incapable of the spontaneous warmth of personality which is so necessary in this work.

One of the most intricate problems lies in the fact that work of this kind attracts men and women who have not themselves come to terms with their own character disorders: the sadist, the canter, the overt or latent homosexual, the psychopath and psychoneurotic. Many such individuals have a good presence, an easy command of language and the acceptable jargon, and may be intelligent and well-read. They make a good impression on committee members and officials who do not possess the child's instinctive aversion for gross, though hidden, personality faults and spurious emotional postures. Once such individuals get into a school it is extremely difficult to unseat them for they need the school infinitely more than the school needs them. Paradoxically, the school environment may keep such an individual from an actual personal breakdown, thus both undermining the therapeutic environment for the child and, at the same time, preventing the adult concerned from coming to terms with his own emotional illness.

The third negative attitude which is occasionally encountered is that of the adult who finds the school for maladjusted children an ideal vehicle for his sadistic need to humiliate others. It is never difficult to humiliate the emotionally disturbed child. He already despises himself, feels helpless and ashamed, and tends to court humiliation and censure. I once heard a teacher tell a boy to go and fetch a broom. When the child returned he was told: 'Now sweep Charlie out of the room. That is what we do with dirt!'

To treat a child in this fashion is inexcusable. Less vicious, but equally humiliating, is the habit of the headmaster of one such school who punishes big boys who run away by making them wear short trousers for a month. If the environment humiliates the child or holds him up to ridicule then it is a simple matter for him to project hatred outward on to his environment because a real external hurt has been done to him. In this situation he can organize himself defensively against an outwardly felt hostility which has a real basis in fact. From the clinical point of view this makes treatment exceedingly difficult because, when the environment offers the child an actual humiliation around which he can crystallize his anger, he uses this as a defence against his unconscious sense of guilt. Unless the child can get in touch with this inner sense of guilt, can face the anxiety it produces, and then slowly recover, it is not possible for him to build up a fully balanced personality.

The fourth type of evasion of conflict which takes place in members of the staff is that of 'impersonal withdrawal'. Some who have been employed at Bredinghurst over short periods have had a singular capacity to view the child with a strange impersonality, as though they were dealing not with lively and disturbed children, so much as with complicated pieces of machinery which from time to time behave in an unreliable fashion. Thus, when faced with a testing situation, the adult is unable to react with an answering anger or strength, or firmness, but merely withdraws into a rather puzzled distance, which inevitably leaves the child completely at a loss, as though finding himself caught in a world of shadows and half-persons.

It is essential in this type of work that a child should be able to feel he is in an environment which is controlled by adults who can behave towards him as people possessed of normal emotions, of genuine attachments, ordinary anger, yet considerable compassion. Given these qualities in the adults who manage a child, it is normally possible for both the child and the adult to meet a testing situation without one or both of them feeling overwhelmed or deprived. It is also possible for both the child and the adult to put the whole episode into perspective in such a way that the resulting relationship between them is more mature, more alive and more meaningful. It must be clear to the child throughout the whole experience that the adult is completely in charge of the situation, in an impregnable position, and also perfectly capable of leading a life of his own which cannot be undermined or threatened by the child's disturbance.

The fifth and most common negative attitude which militates against recovery is that of the disciplinarian who believes that with strong regimentation and control the child can be compelled to behave in a socially acceptable manner, and that this enforced 'goodness' and conformity will gradually become second nature to him. We are convinced that enforced discipline of this kind is only a technique for disguising emotional illness in the child and suppressing his symptoms. No branch of medicine acts on the assumption that to eradicate a symptom is tantamount to a cure of the disease. A symptom is viewed as a signpost to illness not as the disease itself. In this connection D. W. Winnicott writes:[5] 'Most delinquents are to some extent ill . . . and the word illness becomes appropriate through the fact that in many cases the sense of security did not come early enough to be incorporated into his beliefs. While under strong management an anti-social child may seem to be all right; but give him freedom and he soon feels the threat of madness. So he offends against society (without knowing what he is doing) in order to re-establish control from outside.'

We cannot claim to cure delinquency until we can show that the techniques we adopt have the effect of enabling the child to establish control from within, so that the individual does not have, in later life, to appeal to the prison to protect him from his fears of madness.

One disciplinary problem that has given rise to more disagreement between the teaching, house, and psychiatric staff than any other is running-away. How should it be viewed? Should the boys be punished? And if so, how?

It has always seemed to me a great pity that teachers and house-staff should regard running-away as a cardinal crime. One can well understand that when a boy is out of school, possibly running along busy streets or trying to jump a train, or breaking into a house to obtain food or money, the teacher will be anxious. To punish a boy on return may give the adult some relief for his anger and anxiety; he may also believe that it reduces the boy's inclination to repeat the escapade though, in fact, the converse is the case. Running-away is so essential and inevitable a part in the long process of recovery and encountered with such regularity that one had hoped a more philosophical attitude would have been adopted before now.

Obviously it is easier for the psychiatric staff to be philosophical

---

5. *The Child and the Outside World*, Tavistock, London, 1957, p.185.

on this point since they will not be held to blame by irate and worried parents, nor do they have to give up leisure time to fetch a child back from some distant police station. Nevertheless the therapist cannot help but regard running-away as a sign of dependence on, and hope in, the school rather than as a symptom of revolt or blind independence.

There are two elements here: first, running-away becomes a positive experience for the child when he can bring himself to believe that the school staff care sufficiently for him to go and look for him as soon as he is missing, to report his absence to the police and his parents if he is away any length of time, and be willing to take him back into the school on his return. That the school should not merely tolerate him, but actually want him and be eager to fetch him back, may be the child's first convincing proof that anyone really cares for him. To run away, therefore, is a means of testing out the sincerity of the staff, and to find assurance that each individual child is never forgotten or overlooked.

For this reason virtually every boy runs away at one time or another. These are not attempts to escape permanently, though some boys will insist that they are going to hide up so that they will never be found. They are tests of the school's capacity to maintain its interest in the child while he is away, and to seek for him and bring him back at the earliest opportunity.

> In the course of a prolonged period of extremely disturbed behaviour Arthur frequently ran away from the school. On each occasion when he returned he would complain bitterly that if only he had had more luck he would never have been found and brought back to 'this bloody dump'. Gradually, however, he started to come back on his own after a few hours' absence.
>
> On one occasion he allowed himself to be seen leaving the school gates. One of the teachers saw him going and ran downstairs and up to the gate but by then Arthur was nowhere to be seen. The teacher was convinced, however, that he was still within earshot, and so walked along the road calling the boy's name. After a few minutes he decided that there was no point in going further, so he began to walk back into the school to get his car to go looking for him. Just as he was turning into the gate he heard Arthur calling out: 'If you want me, you'll bloody well have to come and get me!' Turning round, the teacher saw the boy on the roof of a nearby house from

where he had been watching the search for him getting under way. He was soon persuaded to come down and return to school.

An instance of this kind clearly illustrates my contention that when boys run away from the school, they seldom have any intention of going for good. It is of great value to them to know that the adults in the school will do everything in their power to get them back.

But why must the maladjusted child choose so dramatic a way of testing out the school's concern for him? This leads to the second element we have to counter: the institutionalized child has no recourse but to make dramatic gestures in circumstances in which the normal child at home does not need to do so. In the ordinary home the child who feels sad or withdrawn need only sit quietly in a passive mood and his mother or father will immediately note that something is amiss. The parent may then ask what is the trouble and give him the special care and consideration he needs for that moment. Or the child may merely withdraw to the privacy of his own bedroom and there gradually recover from his mood. But in an institution there is little privacy and even if the child does go up to his bedroom someone will brusquely ask what he thinks he is doing there when he ought to be in school or on the playing-field.

If the child merely withdraws inside himself he is thought only to be quiet and particularly amenable and no special attention is paid to him. In order to get the understanding and attention which the normal child gets easily in his home, the institutionalized child has to do something dramatic which will focus attention on him – he must run away, or steal, or be aggressive.

To punish him for taking the only course open to him is not only unjust, it also disregards the child's appeal for special consideration and concern. So far from punishing the child who runs away or steals, the duty of the school is to find time to talk with him about what is troubling him. The child may not be able to verbalize his feelings, but at least the sympathy and tolerant understanding of the staff will not be lost on him and some form of genuine communication will have been established.

Both over-permissiveness and over-control as forms of discipline are, rightly, understood by the child as reactions inspired by fear on the part of the adult. Where an individual is afraid of a situation he may either try to establish early control by self-assertion (harsh discipline), or else he may offer no resistance and merely allow himself to be carried along by the tide of feeling in others (overpermissiveness). Thus, both these forms of discipline not only lack a proper affection for the child but are also forms of moral cowardice, signs of a very low threshold of anxiety-tolerance in the adult.

Once the child detects fear of him in the adult environment he is automatically deflected from the essential task for which these schools exist: the inward exploration of his own anxieties, defences, and emotional distortions. It is easier for the maladjusted child to come to terms with hatred in his environment than it is to come to terms with fear. Fear only produces panic in the child and, inevitably, this results in activity to relieve the panic, and the only way the delinquent knows of finding this form of diversionary relief is through delinquent or violent acts. Thus both the restrictive-punitive and the permissive organization actually tend to precipitate in the child the very condition they are designed to prevent.

Discipline, on the other hand, which is built upon a mature conception of love and fearlessness of the child permits him always to stay related to his own problem and not become enmeshed in that of the adults. It provides him with just that admixture of tolerance and firmness against which he can test his own strength and correct the false premises upon which a faulty childhood setting compelled him to set up defensive character formations. From the therapist's point of view it establishes the ideal milieu in which to work creatively, for he can depend upon the other adults in the school to possess not less courage and fortitude than his own, nor less awareness to the child's essential needs. This form of discipline becomes the answer to the child's need for discovering the limits of reality, which alone leads to a stable ego-structuration.

6

Communication

BOTH maladjustment and delinquency may be defined as a partial breakdown in communication. Some vital link between the internal and the external world has been lost. Anti-social behaviour is the outward expression of an inner despair of ever being understood by the environment. It is also an appeal on the part of the child to the environment to find ways of helping him understand himself (insight) and so arrive at integration.

The therapeutic process in a school such as Bredinghurst may, then, be considered as a technique of laying down new lines of communication which make understanding possible. Communication must be established in three dimensions:

between members of the staff;
between the child and adults in normal activities;
between the child and the therapist in the analytical setting.

If any group of adults is to work jointly in a given situation some real measure of mutual understanding, tolerance, and criticism must be striven for. There is a need for a constant interchange of ideas, viewpoints, and information. As I have mentioned earlier, at Bredinghurst this has been achieved to a considerable extent in the formal conferences which are held every Wednesday. But meaningful communication cannot be limited to one period nor one special setting. If the staff are to understand one another and feel that they are each contributing to a central task there must be daily interchanges between them of minute impressions, observations on the children, and reports of small incidents which may have some bearing upon the life of the school, the predicament of an individual child, or his home situation.

Conversation inevitably involves criticism. It is necessary, therefore, in such a school that the adults shall each be sufficiently mature as to be able to withstand and benefit from the criticism of other workers. Given a general climate of goodwill and friendliness this is not difficult to achieve, though it would be absurd and unreal to imply that it is ever possible for so diverse a group of individuals to work together entirely without friction or deep-set disagreement. The free exchange of information does, however, do much to mitigate the suspicion inherent in the different personal disciplines and in the characters and personalities of the individuals concerned. It also enables each member of the staff to gain a daily impression of the children in whom he is specially interested, one that is not bounded exclusively by his own observation, training and experience.

From the therapist's point of view he is kept in close touch with the behaviour of a boy at times when he is not under his direct observation. He gleans information about the child's conduct in school and in the cottage, and is always up-to-date with events and personalities in the boy's home. Teachers and house-staff also benefit from information and impressions which the therapist is able to convey and which can help them in their handling of the child in the context of class and cottage.

> Howard had seemed to be making good progress and had been giving little cause for anxiety to the staff. Suddenly he began to run away with disconcerting regularity, to be abusive and truculent. He told me that he was anxious about his mother's health and that, sometime in the near future, she would have to go into hospital for an operation. The psychiatric social worker confirmed that this was so and I told the headmaster that Howard's present behaviour must be linked with his anxieties about his mother's health.
>
> Eventually his mother was admitted to hospital for a period of observation during which time it was to be determined if an operation was necessary. This meant that, for the time being, Howard was unable to go home at week-ends and his disturbed behaviour increased. Unfortunately at the same time I was absent, ill for a week, and returned to find that Howard had been running

away constantly and no one could discover where he had been going. In a desperate attempt to keep him in the school he had been kept in bed for a day and then, for two further days, had been allowed to roam around the grounds in his pyjamas. This certainly had the effect of keeping him within bounds but did nothing to ease his anxiety nor explain where he had gone or what he had done when he had run away.

His behaviour during my absence had been wild and he was extremely hostile to the staff. My own illness coinciding with his mother's admission to hospital, the boy felt deprived of the support and security which he had enjoyed both at home and in the school, and he was on tenterhooks of anxiety about us both.

On my first day back at work I saw him for an hour and he broke down in floods of tears, told me of his fears for my life and also of his terror that his mother also would die. He had been unable to sleep, had eaten little and passed each day in a feverish state of foreboding. He also told me that when he ran away he had always gone immediately to a local cemetery. There he had found a partly dug grave in an out-of-the-way corner, had roofed it over with branches and scraps of tarpaulin and would sit for hours among the graves thinking of his mother. He drew a map of the cemetery for me so that if news came through that his mother had had her operation or had died I would be able to find him and tell him the news. He could not bear, he said, to be in the school surrounded by boys who were not in touch with his anxiety, while he was longing all the time just to be alone with his anxious thoughts.

In his hide-out in the cemetery he had concealed a knife, a sheet of paper and an envelope, a pencil, a box of matches and a candle. If his mother died under the operation he intended to write a letter to me and another to his father and then to slash his wrists.

Once I had conveyed the tenor of this conversation to the headmaster and the boy's cottage-mother they no longer felt any need to take action to prevent his running away, which he continued to do until the day of the operation. Once the operation was over and his mother's recovery assured his behaviour return to normal.

In many less dramatic but equally significant ways the daily interchange of information and impressions serves to supplement the work of each member of the staff.

In the main a natural and easy relationship between the children and the staff is deliberately fostered in the school. Once it is accepted that the role of the teacher and house-mother must conform as nearly as possible to that of the parent in the home, it is obvious that the members of the staff must be, above everything else, available.

These children are not public-school boys coming from good and stable homes. They are not likely to respond to, nor recover in, an atmosphere which demands high standards of hygiene, excruciating good-manners, and a 'Sir' in every sentence. The teacher or house-parent who stands on his dignity, preserves an air of aloof superiority, or tries to introduce a semi-military régime has no real appreciation of the delicacy nor the intricate nature of the task. If he is easily upset by a nickname or given to a display of moral indignation at the sound of a swear word, there must be a place in the educational system for him elsewhere. If, on the other hand, the adult is genuinely kindly, uncensorious, and infinitely available he will earn the child's warm affection and respect even though he may have to grow accustomed to finding these sentiments expressed in unconventional ways and language.

For the truly interested and imaginative teacher or house-parent each day presents a hundred opportunities for valuable contact and exchange with the boys in his care. In the playground, in class, at meal-times, in the showers, in bed at night, in any natural situation there are openings for meaningful conversation with the children, openings which the children themselves are only too eager to exploit. For if the maladjusted child makes one thing patently clear it is that he wants to talk. He may not at first know how to talk, or he may distrust those who are willing to listen, or he may hide meaningful communications beneath a welter of superficial conversation. But once he feels secure, assured of the goodwill of the adult, and certain that he will not run into immediate condemnation, there is virtually nothing he will not discuss or reveal.

It is interesting, too, to note that these children do not resent the staff talking about them among themselves. They know that this kind of conversation goes on all the time, as it would between normal parents in a normal house, and they take this as a sure sign of the adults' interest in and concern for them. They are often openly grateful to know that they are being discussed in conference and that a file is kept in the office on each boy, in which are collected medical, educational, and psychiatric reports. It should also be observed that the children talk freely among themselves not only about the staff but about each other and are sometimes able to make incisive judgements on one another.

The adult worker who feels it his duty is to enforce a particular moral outlook on the child, and who uses the quiet and relaxed moments which occur with the children to impose his point of view, never really gains his confidence. The capacity to bear quietness, to tolerate the withdrawn mood of the child, and to wait for him to take the first steps towards real communication is one of the most valuable assets in any worker with maladjusted children. Given this patient and imaginative quality it is possible for the adult to listen intently, observe accurately, and move cautiously in intimacy with the child's deeply felt, but dimly perceived, predicament.

When sufficient members of the staff are capable of this subtle form of detached identification with the child he can sense that the adults provide a 'screen' on to which he can project his ideas, fantasies and anxieties, and test these out against the standards and values of adults whom he can admire and of whose sincerity and affection there is no doubt.

While each member of the staff takes over at some time one or other aspect of the parental role in relation to the boys (transference), it is only the therapist who is able to interpret and relate to past experience the significance of these reactions and feelings. Undoubtedly the special quality of this relationship between child and therapist becomes the dynamic element in the treatment of the more disturbed children. Fortunately, as we have seen, the boys take it for granted that much of their behaviour and conversation will be reported back to the therapist. They do not, on the whole, regard this as a betrayal of confidence and do, in fact, expect of the therapist that he see each boy in as wide a context as possible. On the other hand the therapist has to be circumspect about what information he gleans in the analytical setting and is wise if he first seeks leave from his patients if he has any special information which he wishes to convey to other members of the staff.

The children recognize from the first that the therapeutic hour is something additional to and outside of the ordinary management of the school and confidences given in this setting will not be betrayed to teachers and house-staff who might take up a punitive attitude. The therapist is usually told by his patients what boys intend to run away and why, who has been stealing, who is responsible for damage done to school property and so on. If he immediately fed this information back to the school staff he would, quite rightly, be regarded as misusing his privileged position and would in a large measure undo the therapeutic purpose of the session.

The relationship between the child and the therapist is something that most mature teachers and house-staff accept and in the main they do nothing to interfere with the process. Occasionally, however, non-psychiatric staff have sought to decry the value of the analytical approach in conversation with other staff members or with the boys themselves. Most often these hostile gestures are a transparent manœuvre designed to ward off personal anxiety occasioned by dismay at discovering how intricate a problem these children present. Nevertheless it is possible to hold the sincere opinion that analytical techniques are not fitted to the treatment of the maladjusted child, but such opinions should not of course be aired with the children themselves who need to grasp at every possible chance of help and understanding open to them.

Adults working in close association on a joint task have the right to expect tolerance and support from all their colleagues. The teacher who seeks to undermine the position of the therapist in the school is making an unwarranted attack upon the creativity of another and, at the same time, exposing himself to the accusation that he has a precarious trust in his own discipline.

Less easy to deal with and rather more pernicious is the attitude of the teacher or house-parent who falsely assumes that psychotherapy is 'mere talk' and its efficacy based solely upon an ability to get a child to 'talk about his worries'. This false assessment of the analytical process and technique inclines certain workers to believe that, without special training, they can produce startling cures and to claim the credit for a child's improvement. These individuals are totally unaware of the intricacy of the problem they so blithely aim to investigate and are unaware of the harm they can do in the process.

Alongside the need for a continual interchange of viewpoints and experiences it is true to say that the stability and success of the school depend to a large degree on the capacity of each worker to keep circumspectly within his prescribed role and not to invade the territory of his colleagues. As time goes on I am confident that with higher standards in special education this type of interference will gradually cease. It must be part of the experimental process that some confusion of roles takes place before a clear understanding of, and respect for, the role played by each member of the team is arrived at. The need for all the staff to work without crippling envy alongside colleagues with disparate qualifications, experience, and therapeutic roles is essential. It depends in the last resort upon the willingness of everyone to accept that however important the role he may play, the child's ultimate restoration can be achieved only with the help of other workers whose duties and functions complement his own.

7

Inter-Staff Tensions

WHETHER one's point of view is conditioned by professional training, or whether one chooses a particular training to support an ingrained bias, the result is the same. The diversity of the personal disciplines among the staff in a school necessarily results in intellectual positions which are frequently at variance. It is difficult for the educationist not to sympathize with the notion that wrong actions are the product of wilful disobedience on the part of a child and, as such, deserve condign punishment. The therapist, on the other hand, chooses to look beyond the conscious act to unconscious motives and is frequently accused, while being engrossed in this concern, of neglecting the child's responsibility for his misdemeanour.

A few examples of the manner in which the therapist and the schoolmaster may clash must suffice. I have already mentioned that disagreement arises over the perennial problem of running-away. The child knows that he is not supposed to take leave of absence in this way and may show this by the furtive manner in which he plans his escape. To the teacher this is a clear indication of the child's deliberate wish to revolt against authority. It is carefully planned, consciously executed and, therefore, should be treated as a violation of the school rules.

The therapist on the other hand is aware that running-away may be the only manner in which a child can overcome a profound sense of emotional stupor or 'deadness': he escapes from his inner lethargy, temporarily, with the aid of vivid and exciting adventure. It may, as I suggested earlier, be an indication that he has reached a point in his development where he needs to test the school's declared concern for him. That he is missed from the group, that a teacher or house-father sets out to look for him, that the police and his parents are informed of his absence, that every practical measure is taken to fetch him back are all valuable indications to the child that the adults in his environment are anxious about him.

If any of these motives lies at the back of the event the therapist is bound to feel that anything more than perfunctory punishment is out of place. Whatever is done on the child's return should not injure or threaten the relationship which made the escapade possible for and significant to the child. Not unnaturally, the teaching and house-staff tend to think that this attitude is unreal, does not give proper place to the natural anxiety of the workers, and is tenable by the therapist only because he does not have to bear full responsibility for the day-to-day care of the child. At various times certain members of the teaching staff have not only severely punished the boy who runs away, but have gone to considerable lengths to prevent his leaving the premises.

While the psychiatric team have no wish to encourage truancy in any child, nor support lax discipline, which might be interpreted by the child as lack of interest, they feel that severe punishment is out of place as is any form of control which humiliates, or rigidly restrains a child's movements. Confinement to bed is bound to be viewed by the child as an infantile and humiliating form of punishment or prevention of crime, besides increasing sexual tension and cutting him off from the normal life of the school. Most humiliating of all has been the habit of a few teachers to keep a boy in his pyjamas though allowing him to attend school in the usual way. One boy was permitted to dress, save for his trousers, and for a period of two weeks attended school half-clad, an object of ridicule to the rest of the school. The therapist cannot but view such an action as a gross assault on the child, on his developing sexuality and sense of identity. He sees in it an unconscious sexual assault on the boy's genitality since it is bound to be experienced by the child as a castrating act.

The second example of open conflict between the teaching and psychiatric staff which I wish to describe in some detail is that which can arise from the general attitude to sexuality. The analytically trained individual regards sexuality as a normal and necessary part of the psychic make-up of the child. He is not horrified by sexual swearing, by masturbation or sex-play between adolescent boys. He would be more concerned rather than less if there were no evidence of sexual interest or excitement in the children. Teaching and house-staff, however, are inclined to be disturbed by these things. The house-mothers particularly tend to regard sexuality with a certain distaste.

When we first began working at Bredinghurst we had to dissuade some of the women members of the staff from punishing boys for masturbating or 'playing with one another'. Some of the house-mothers felt it to be their duty to lecture children detected in these activities on the supposed dangers of masturbation to their physical and mental health. Yet these same women were so unaware of their own sexuality and of the boys' need for privacy they felt free to walk into the dormitories when adolescent children were undressing, or to supervise them while in the bath or showers. One woman went so far as to punish a twelve-year-old boy by making him take off all his clothes in front of her and then sending him up to bed where he was not permitted to wear even his pyjamas for two days. When I suggested to her that the boy could only regard this as a sexual assault at the very onset of adolescence, she remarked blandly, offended: 'But I've seen lots of boys undressed. That sort of thing doesn't interest me. They're only children after all.'

Much of what the therapist welcomes as improvement in the development of a child, his increased liveliness, his sexual assertion, boisterous behaviour, a liking for ostentatious modes of dress and hair-style, is customarily regarded by teaching or house-staff as yet another sign of depravity or tiresome unruliness. It is important to note that the therapist does not sanction or encourage bad behaviour. Disobedience and unpalatable conduct and attitudes are no part of the analytical technique and have, in themselves, no therapeutic value. What is necessary, however, is to recognize and allow for a wish (a process) in the child which may articulate itself in behaviour that has certain latent disturbing elements. The teacher may disapprove of the overt action if he chooses, so long as he also keeps in mind the positive element behind the action that is in tune with the child's developing ego-structure.

From time to time certain members of the house-staff insisted on complete silence at meal-times. They argued that since they have to share their meals with the boys they have the right to eat in reasonable quietness and peace, and since a group of fifteen boys are inclined to chatter excitedly if allowed to talk at all, the only alternative is complete and monastic silence. Here again the psychiatric staff have offered criticism, pointing out that silence at mealtimes destroys absolutely the social aspect of eating. In a healthy family talking and eating together enforce the sense of 'belonging' and of excited taking in to the self of good things provided and prepared by affectionate adults. To deny the child this experience is to give him good food but to make the experience indigestible by creating a hostile atmosphere.

In the early years much disagreement took place between the house- and psychiatric staff over the question of good manners. Certain workers insisted that a large part of our responsibility to the boys in our care was to inculcate in them the social graces, and were particularly distressed to find that, unless constantly schooled, the maladjusted child seldom showed gratitude for the enormous amount of hard work that the staff undertook for him. The maladjusted child is as likely to say: 'Well, you're paid for it, aren't you?' as he is to say 'Thank you'. The man or woman who needs immediate recognition for the work he does finds this attitude hard to bear. They feel that the object to whom they do good must recognize that goodness has been done. These workers tend to insist on party manners or respectful modes of address, on consideration, and the rights of the adult in order that they may get some satisfaction from the arduous tasks which are imposed on them.

What they do not easily recognize is that every deprived child has good and solid reason to doubt the motives of the adults around him, and it may be years before he is able to realize with what devotion his needs have been met. It may take an equally long time for these adults to appreciate that a child may show gratitude not by verbal acknowledgement, but by an increasing capacity to accept and digest good experiences and to find a true measure of health. This is the ultimate reward for the adult.

The therapist starts from the position where symptoms are viewed as signposts to an inner need; and unless this inner need is understood and met we have failed the child exactly at the point of hope. In several of his recent papers Dr D. W. Winnicott has emphasized this point of view. He says, for instance: 'The anti-social tendency is characterized by *an element in it which compels the environment to be important.* The patient through unconscious drives compels someone to attend to management. It is the task of the therapist to become involved in this patient's unconscious drive, and the work is done by the therapist in terms of management, tolerance, and understanding. *The anti-social tendency implies hope*. . . .'[1] In another place, he writes: 'Anti-social behaviour is at times no more than an S.O.S. for control by strong, loving, confident people.'[2]

This being so the therapist is bound to view anti-social behaviour as a child's appeal to an environment of whose capacity for understanding he has not yet despaired. He hopes, and half-believes, that this environment will be able to hold, sustain, and protect him against himself and, if necessary, against society until such time as he has been able to reorganize his feeling life around mature adults and mature standards and values, and to tolerate his inner conflicts.

The task of therapy with the maladjusted child may be said to be: to aim at enabling the child to build up an inner world of cogent affective experiences and meaningful internal objects and relationships.[3]

> John, a boy of fourteen, who had a long history of petty thieving, mostly from home, told me that he had a dream in which he and two other boys decided to raid a local bank in Peckham. In the dream they carried out the robbery successfully and, each with a bag of gold in his hand, jumped into a car which was waiting to drive them away with their swag. To their surprise, when they clambered into the car, they found that the driver was the headmaster of Bredinghurst. He drove them back to the school, returned them to their classes, and also arranged for the gold to be returned to the bank.
>
> I interpreted this dream, in part, on the lines that John was beginning to hope that the school would be able to help him handle his delinquency and that it contained a very positive element of confidence and trust in the school. I was also able to warn the teaching and house-staff that John would very probably begin to steal more openly and that we might be in for a difficult period with the boy who had, to that time, appeared docile and co-operative.
>
> A week later John and two other boys absconded from the school, broke into a number of houses, stole a great many articles, including two bicycles, and were apprehended and charged by the police after a week of almost constant delinquency.

1. *Collected Papers*. Tavistock, London, 1958, p.309.
2. *The Child and the Outside World*. Tavistock, London, 1957, p.185.
3. cf. Klein, M. *Psycho-analysis of Children*. Hogarth, London, 1932, p.36f.

It was possible in this instance to persuade the school authorities that this was a dramatic gesture of hope on the part of the boys concerned, and to prevail on the juvenile court to leave them in our care. As Winnicott has stated: 'The understanding that the anti-social act is an expression of hope is vital in the treatment of children who show the anti-social tendency. Over and over again one sees the moment of hope wasted, or withered, because of mismanagement or intolerance.'[4]

Without convincing psychiatric support it is virtually inevitable that the 'moment of hope' will be viewed by the pure educationist as no more than a perverse act of the delinquent mind; punishment will be meted out, or the school or the court may conclude that the child needs to be placed in an approved school. The child, as so often happens, is then summarily removed from the one setting in which he has any confidence, and which he had a half-formed hope would be able to bear with him over a critical and vital phase. The dashing of his hopes at this point may finally seal off any possibility of cure.

The tension that exists between the therapist and the tutorial staff stems from this fundamental divergence of views, though it is only fair to add that, in a very large measure, normally imaginative and concerned teachers and house-staff are able to reconcile themselves with the therapeutic approach.

So long as these schools are administered solely by the education authorities the position of the therapist will remain a difficult one, for it is always for the headmaster or administration to act in ways detrimental to the therapeutic process, without consultation with the psychiatric team. The latter have to rely solely upon their ability to persuade the headmaster to take into consideration the therapeutic point of view. At Bredinghurst this has usually been possible. From time to time, however, certain decisions with far-reaching consequences were taken without our knowledge or in the face of our keenest protests. Sometimes a boy was discharged when it was our reasoned conviction that he should be kept in the school for a longer period. Administrative changes were instituted or methods of punishment employed which we felt would be damaging to the child's emotional development.

These reverses the psychiatric team may take hardly since they are responsible for the emotional health of the children and believe

4. Winnicott, D. W., *Collected Papers*, p.309.

themselves to be in closer touch with the children's inner needs and more sensible of the effect on the pulse of the school of one decision or another. The traditional distrust of the 'expert' and the specialist may be an amusing trait in the British character when viewed in the abstract. But it is less amusing for the specialist himself, who has learned both theoretically and empirically the adverse effects of a certain situation, and who is obliged to accept decisions which he knows can only prejudice his work and the health of the children in treatment. Neither the ordinary teacher nor the professional administrator is likely to have sufficient knowledge of maladjustment to arrive at a positive decision, and unless they are willing to confer with the therapeutic staff gross errors are easily made. We shall return to this aspect of the problem in our later chapter on Recommendations.[5]

The situation is ameliorated for the psychiatric team by the knowledge that though they themselves may prefer a certain type of environment for the child, they cannot expect teaching and house-staff to assume responsibilities or support anxieties which they appear to be unwilling to bear or are constitutionally incapable of compassing. The handling and treatment of maladjusted children places a very heavy burden of emotional strain on all the staff, not least because these children act in ways which are designed to evoke hatred in adults. Unless a high level of good-feeling and mutual respect exists between the adults, and unless members of the staff can come to terms with the hatred engendered in themselves, positive work is impossible. One of the latent dangers of a school of this kind is that the unacknowledged hatred aroused by the behaviour of the patients may easily become a dislocating force between various members of the staff. The need for tolerably good staff-relationships is therefore paramount, not only so that the boys are not disturbed by the equivalent in the school setting of inter-parental divisions, but also that the staff themselves can survive the severe stresses to which they will inevitably be exposed.

One great danger in a school of this kind is the tendency to confuse the roles of the various adult workers. It is not expected, for example, that teachers should attempt to carry out therapy. The teacher or house-parents who will sit an anxious or depressed child on his lap and ask him with a supposedly professional air to 'tell me all your worries' may earnestly wish to help the boy. It is,

5. See p.168.

however, nothing more than a particularly unfortunate attempt to usurp the role of the therapist since the teacher does not have the skill to take advantage of a mechanically contrived situation such as this, even supposing it were a positive method of establishing meaningful communication between a child and an adult. Actions of this kind on the part of the educational or child-care staff point to an unconscious envy of the therapist's role and, perhaps, a lack of faith in the dynamic of education. Moreover, there is the very real danger of the stimulation of sexual fantasies which may easily result in damaging accusations against the teacher and have grave consequences for the school itself. Unless each member of the staff can know with some clarity, and observe with circumspection, the spheres in which his personality bears upon the child and so keep himself and his function distinct from that of other adult workers, the child will be subjected to great anxiety and clinical work handicapped.

8

Distrust of Psychotherapy

PIONEER work of any kind is bound to meet hostility from the settled interests of those who have, till the present, been dealing with the situation. Suspicion, both social and individual, is never lacking towards those who adopt new methods. In psychotherapy there is the additional hazard that psycho-analytical techniques are generally felt as a personal threat by those who are doubtful of the premises upon which their own work is constructed, or are unconsciously aware of the precarious balance of their personal emotional equilibrium.

It is to the credit of the headmaster of Bredinghurst that he sought, from the first, to incorporate a psychiatric unit within his school and gave the team every possible support, though he was well aware that this would involve much rethinking about his own position and the attempt to establish a system that would be both workable and embrace an apparently alien discipline. The conscious acceptance of a new discipline is, however, a very different thing from a complete embracement of all that psychotherapy implies. That the school not only survived this grafting operation (of psychotherapy on to education) but actually became a more creative medium reflects well upon all those who joined in the experiment. It may be stated categorically that without a high degree of maturity and adaptability on the part of all the staff it would not have been possible to establish a truly therapeutic environment.

Even given this situation, it is inevitable that the latent hostility to psychotherapy from those who have not themselves been analysed is bound to show itself in a variety of ways which complicate the work of the therapeutic team. This threat may come from any or all of four different sources: the school staff, the parents, the central administration, and the courts.

In the ordinary school the role of the headmaster is a relatively simple one. He has to administer an educational machine for the advantage of children who have good home-backgrounds and satisfactory relationships with their parents. In a school for maladjusted children, however, the headmaster has a particularly complicated role. He has not only to be the administrator and co-ordinator. He also becomes for each child in the school a father-figure to a greater or lesser extent. This, intuitively, is what every good headmaster allows himself to become in such circumstances. 'Without one person to love and to hate he (the child) cannot come to know that it is one person that he loves and hates, and so cannot find his sense of guilt, and his desire to repair and restore. Unless he can know a limited physical and human environment he cannot find out the extent to which his aggressive ideas actually fail to destroy, and so cannot sort out the difficulty between fantasy and fact.'[1] It is vitally important for the child, therefore, that the headmaster be a strong, positive, imaginative yet tolerant human being who, without self-conscious deliberation, can act in a natural and warm manner towards the children in his charge.

The fact that he cares for them as individuals is the secret of his success but it also means that he feels it as a personal deprivation if some of these children establish an even more intense dependency, over a period at least, on the therapist. Headmasters are human beings after all and it is not easy, even for the best of them, to discover that another member of the staff has a deeper understanding of a child than he himself possesses, and that the child appears to have established a new constellation of intense emotions around the therapist. The fact that the child can do this is, of course, simply because he can take the headmaster's continued indulgence and concern for granted. This is, in consequence, a measure of the head's understanding and humanity. But the headmaster may not always be able to view things in this way. Natural jealousy may explain why sometimes a headmaster will act out of character and make a decision which gravely affects the work of the therapist, or may discharge a boy at a time when it is obvious to the therapist or psychiatrist that to do so is likely to prejudice the work of months or even years of treatment, and that the child's trust will be tragically shattered.

Until such time as the authorities see fit to appoint to these

1. Winnicott, D. W., *The Child and the Outside World*. Tavistock, London, 1957, p.102.

schools headmasters and teachers who have specialized education and some experience in the handling of disturbed children it is inevitable that much damage will be done to the therapeutic processes within the school, not from malice but from unconscious motivations or bias.

On a somewhat similar plane this bias is encountered among the house-staff who, understandably, sometimes feel that the important role they play in the management of the child is not fully appreciated. For many years yet it will not be practical to hope that house-staff will be selected from among well-educated sections of the community – nor would it necessarily be an advantage if they were. The qualities in house-fathers and house-matrons that are of most value to the child – tolerance, strength, spontaniety, warm humanity, imagination, gentleness – are qualities which are by no means the special possession of the better educated. In the main the homely philosophy and relaxed matter-of-fact attitude of the house-staff provide the most suitable atmosphere for the disturbed child. Most of the staff who worked at Bredinghurst were willing to discuss freely with the members of the psychiatric team their own difficulties in the work, took a lively interest in the problems the boys presented, and willingly accepted what advice was given.

Occasionally, however, the hostility, conscious or unconscious, of certain workers gave rise to sudden, though brief crises. One house-matron, for example, developed the habit of asking the boys in her cottage who were in treatment, what they had been discussing that day with 'The Dream Doctor'. This appellation in itself was sufficient to indicate to the children that her interest was critical rather than sympathetic, hostile not academic. If they told her something of what had taken place in the session she made derisive comments on the material and on the interpretations the therapist was supposed to have made. Fortunately she quickly decided that she had little contribution to make to the school and sought another post.

It is a comforting reflection that, provided the men and women appointed to this kind of work have a certain evenness of temperament, a genuine concern to do well by the boys and a capacity to learn, they invariably come to look upon the work they have to do in the school as valuable, positive and rewarding, and ally themselves with the psychiatric team.

. . . . . .

The parents of most of the children we treat have a markedly ambivalent attitude towards their own children. Genuine affection for the child is seldom altogether absent, but running alongside it may be partial rejection, intolerance, overt anxiety or despair. At certain times these parents cannot prevent themselves acting towards the child and the school in such a manner as to damage further their child's chances of recovery.

Most boys who recover pass through a pronounced period of apparent deterioration, irresponsibility, and overt delinquency. We warn the parents that this is likely to happen and that it should be regarded as a positive sign rather than evidence of failure. But at such times the raw anxiety of the parents may so get the upper hand that they remove the child from the school on the grounds that he is being made worse rather than better. If he is on a Fit Person Order they may apply to the court for its revocation, or in some other way give the child the impression that they have removed their support from the work of the school. This, in itself, is sometimes sufficient to precipitate acute anxiety in the child who feels that in beginning to hope he was asking to be betrayed, that just when he has become dependent upon the school and the therapist these things will be snatched from him, that the cost of showing signs of recovery is to be removed from the very people who have made recovery possible.

Some parents become hostile to the school or the therapist when their child shows unmistakable signs of improvement. This may be due to their resentment that someone other than themselves has succeeded where they have failed. The sad thing about such cases is that the child is removed from our care at the highest point of dependence, thus tragically repeating the original trauma of deprivation.

The parents of a maladjusted child inevitably feel guilty that they have failed their child. It is felt by them as a deep humiliation that he should make a more positive attachment to someone outside the home setting, and that this person should be able to lead the child on towards a degree of health which the home could not offer. That this should have been achieved by 'mere talk', and not by powerful drugs or brain surgery, only exacerbates the sense of failure.

Another common cause of hostility from the home is the insistence on the part of the therapist that these children deserve to be understood rather than castigated. A large proportion of parents complain that the discipline in the school is too lax, that their children 'get away' with things, that when they do wrong the headmaster and the therapist go to court to represent the child and plead for his return, and that not enough corporal punishment is given by the staff. For this state of affairs they tend to blame the therapist – and this is probably just.

Nevertheless it should be recorded that usually once the crisis has passed and the parents can themselves see a positive change in the child, can detect an increasing capacity for him to feel at home in the home and to show genuine affection towards them, they are willing to concede, with a certain hint of incredulity, that psychotherapy may have certain advantages over the cane.

The fact has to be faced that there is a strong bias against psychoanalysis in the community at large to which education authorities and County Councils are not immune. As Dr Edward Glover has said, 'Delinquency is essentially a co-efficient of friction between the individual and the community. . . . It is the habit of public administrators and of many child welfare officials to put the convenience of the community before the needs of the individual.'[2] To our way of thinking the chief obstacle in the way of really creative work being done in our schools for maladjusted children is that these schools have sprung out of a well-meaning, but comparatively ill-informed and undefined, social movement. Thus maladjustment and delinquency are viewed as social irritants and not as they should be viewed – as symptoms of personal deprivation and emotional disorder deserving of skilled treatment.

The great drawback for the therapeutic school owned by a local authority is that ultimate responsibility is in the hands of administrators who seldom as yet have any clinical training or experience, who have not worked in the type of school for which they are responsible and have little understanding of the psychodynamic problem. Feeling themselves to be out of their depth in a clinical situation, they are inclined to favour those headmasters who rely upon authoritarian techniques to produce a school in

2. Introduction to Melitta Schmideberg's, *Children in Need*. Allen & Unwin, London, 1948, p.9.

which a superficial orderliness makes it appear that sound remedial work is being done.

This bias on the part of administrators and inspectors can have a cumulatively undermining effect on the headmaster who seeks to work closely with his psychiatric team, for he cannot help but feel that he is losing the wholehearted support of his superiors. Furthermore he can seldom turn to them for counsel or advice because he has become increasingly aware of their lack of knowledge and their thinly veiled hostility to his approach. Nevertheless he has to depend upon the central administration in many practical matters – special equipment, alterations to buildings, recruiting new staff – and if administrative officers have their own doubts about the school's methods there are many ways in which they can affect the running of the school, and also the headmaster's reputation and hopes of advancement in the service.

Fortunately, since these schools depend upon a close working association between the education and public health departments of the County Councils, it should only be a matter of time before the educational administration feels less threatened by the clinical approach, and new administrators and inspectors are appointed whose attitudes are less defensively organized.

In a later chapter we shall return to the delicate problem of the relationship between the psychiatric team and the courts. At this point I wish merely to state that we are still not convinced that many magistrates and probation officers have any real understanding of the significance of analytical techniques. It is our impression that many of them are convinced that the therapeutically orientated school is in league with the child against society, determined to enter into collusion with the child against the law, and so spare him punishment.

This could not be further from the truth. It has always been our contention that nothing is ever gained by shielding a child from the legal implications of his acts, and what measures we may take to prevent his being sent to an approved school are taken because we are convinced that any interruption of his treatment will prejudice his chance of recovery. This attitude we underline to the boy himself. A boy may thank the therapist for 'getting me off' after a court case, but we always step in to say that we have not got him off, but have merely asked the court not to terminate his treatment by precipitate action. The boys are quick to sense that we have the utmost respect for the law and that when we go to court we are by no means sure that our plea will be heard or acted on. They know that the school co-operates with the police and the C.I.D. when any boy has been delinquent, and never allows any child to keep stolen property. The therapist must work for the boy's ultimate good strictly within the framework of the law.

It is undeniable that some magistrates, possibly because they have become disillusioned by seeing so many boys to whom they have given 'one more chance' appear before them again, are inclined to think that the therapist is just a deluded optimist about human nature. They know little or nothing of the school, nor of analytical methods, and not infrequently take advantage of their privileged position to pour scorn on analytical theories or pronounce sentences which either terminate treatment or make its outcome less hopeful. Few professional men are placed, as a therapist repeatedly is, in a position where the work he is doing is held up to public scrutiny long before it is completed. It is not an easy thing to have one's work openly questioned in court by people who have no skill, knowledge or experience which qualifies them to measure the effectiveness of the work done, and who sometimes cannot disguise their distrust of any who regard delinquency as a symptom of distress rather than a deliberate social affront.

For the time being at least the psychotherapist has to work in an environment which is overtly or covertly suspicious of the motives, aims, and methods. He has often to attempt to rescue a boy from the determined and damaging influence of the home, yet he can do this only by holding the boy in a school environment which is, in certain aspects, unwilling or unable to provide the appropriate milieu for treatment, and which is the property of an administration which is still to some extent out of sympathy with him. He has, in addition, to accept for treatment boys who he knows will at some time probably become delinquent and will, in consequence, appear before a bench of magistrates who are not inclined to give the boy much rope nor the therapist much credence! In view of all this it never ceases to amaze us that the great majority of the boys whom we treat recover and are able to take their place in the community as normal, responsible citizens.

9

The Anti-Social Child

ANYONE who undertakes to deal with the maladjusted child must be confronted, sooner or later, with the marked anti-social tendency in these children. All maladjusted children have one thing in common. They have, without exception, experienced a real deprivation in childhood. This is not the same thing as simple privation. It is an actual experience of the loss of a good relationship which once existed between the child and his parents, and around which he has organized an unconscious constellation of affects.[1] Good therapy must provide an environment in which the child can regress, can retrace his emotional development to the point at which the original trauma took place and then, in the therapeutic milieu, establish a meaningful relationship with adults who will not repeat the original deprivation. In this way the child is enabled to get fruitfully in touch with his unconscious conflicts and personal sense of guilt and, hence, his desire to make restitution.

It is not difficult for adults, particularly when motivated by sentimental attitudes about children, to provide a milieu in which the child begins to hope and this hope results in violence, aggression, or stealing. Unfortunately it often happens that the adults fail to understand the unconscious motivations, and regard anti-social behaviour on the child's part as a sign of failure on theirs and, consequently, reject him.

---

1. Nothing strikes the analytically oriented observer (or for that matter anyone looking purely at the phenomenology of delinquent behaviour) more forcibly than the obvious sadistic intention behind the delinquent act. Yet the one affect which the anti-social child cannot personalize is the sadistic component of primitive instinctual life. See Winnicott, D. W., *Collected Papers*: Tavistock, London, 1958, p.145f.

The child who steals or becomes destructive is acting from unconscious motives which give him the right to behave in this way, for he is repeating in adolescent form the original demands which the infant makes on his mother. The infant has a right to take from his mother and he also has a right to expect his mother to be able to provide him with an environment that is secure and affectionate enough to tolerate his excited, lively aggressiveness.[2]

It may be said then that the child who steals is not seeking the object he has stolen, but a person, his mother; and the destructive child is not seeking to wreck his environment but to find his own way through to a sense of liveliness which includes both love and aggression fused in one experience: To the thief it is not the fountain pen from Woolworth's, or the bicycle from the neighbour's railings, or the apple from the orchard, that can give satisfaction. A child who is ill in this way is incapable of enjoying the possession of things stolen. He is only acting out a fantasy which belongs to his primitive love impulses, and the best he can do is to enjoy the acting out, and the skill exercised. The fact is that he has lost touch with his mother in some sense or other. The mother may or may not still be there. She may even be there, and a perfectly good mother, and able to give him any amount of love. From the child's point of view, however, there is something missing. He may be fond of his mother and even in love with her, but, in a more primitive sense, for some reason or other she is lost to him. The child who is thieving is an infant looking for the mother, or for the person *from whom he has the right to steal*; in fact, he seeks the person from whom he can take things, just as, as an infant and a little child of 1 or 2 years old, he took things from his mother simply because she *was* his mother, and because he had rights over her.'[3]

Viewed this way, even stealing and delinquency have their positive aspects. They give the environment a second chance to meet the child's primitive experience of deprivation. If the environment can continue to be tolerant, protective and imaginatively affectionate, many delinquent children can come through to emotional health without individual psychotherapy. The environment is therapy enough. But this can be so only if the environment is able to sense that there are positive elements, as

2. ibid. p.300f.
3. Winnicott, D. W., *The Child and the Outside World*. Tavistock, London, 1957, p.177.

well as the obvious negative ones, in anti-social behaviour and that increasingly disorderly conduct over a period may indicate anxiety consequent upon a loosening of rigid unconscious defence mechanisms.

While the delinquent expects his environment and the community at large to take note of his social conduct, he also harbours an inner hope that retributive action will be taken in such a way as to enable him to get in touch with his personal sense of guilt and the urge to make good. For this reason long moral harangues from teaching or child-care staff following some outbreak of anti-social conduct may, in certain circumstances, actually prevent a child from making positive use of the episode and arriving at a personal feeling of guilt and responsibility.

Thus the anti-social act may be viewed in two ways. First, the delinquent and the maladjusted child is at the mercy of primitive sadistic imagos (super-ego) persecuting the self. From this internal stress the disturbed child finds relief in an anti-social act, thereby inviting the community's censure and punishment. Actual punishment lessens for a time the inordinate tension from guilt and retaliatory fears. The moralist and ordinary educationist react to this situation spontaneously, providing both condemnation and punishment. Almost invariably the child temporarily reacts favourably, punishment being followed by a marked diminution in anxiety and a spell of improved social behaviour. Unfortunately this is often taken to mean that disciplinary measures are curative, which they are not. In time, internal pressures build up in the child again and the whole process has to be repeated.

Secondly, the anti-social act may, by contrast, be viewed as an appeal for help towards completing a range of missed infantile experiences. If so, in anti-social behaviour the child is:

(a) staking a claim,
(b) in hope,
(c) on an environment that should understand.

If in fact the school environment is able to accept this construction and provide the necessary tolerance and understanding it is then clinically possible to make the child aware of his inner primitive conflicts and arrive at his own sense of guilt, an awareness of sadism and love, and hence to make true restitution. If this path can be followed and the child gains the necessary insight, anti-social behaviour does not become repetitive and the boy is able to conform without coercion to normal social and ethical standards.

It is important not to overlook the strength of the maladjusted child's unconscious defence mechanisms, for while he may wish to gain health, be reunited with his family, and renounce delinquent conduct, any real change which might bring him nearer to any of these goals can be achieved only by apparently undermining the fabric of his psychic stability. This is productive of profound anxiety in the child and may give rise to outbursts of violent anger against the therapist or other members of the staff.

The maladjusted child has made many attempts to help himself, following the initial traumatic injustice, and has developed many defensive techniques in relation to this. In certain states his dependence on his self-cure techniques becomes over-determined and any attempt to put him in touch with his original experience of loss is accompanied by real anxiety. The maladjusted child, therefore, carries in him a very intense negative therapeutic force which punitive measures and procedures can all too easily mobilize.

The central aim of all those who deal with the anti-social child may, then, be summed up in one sentence. *It is to act in such a way as to enable the child to get in touch with his personal sense of guilt and his need to make restitution*, rather than to impress on him the condemnation of the community.

This aim cannot be achieved by massive moralizing or punitive measures. In this connection Gregory Zilboorg has written: 'We are all thieves at one time or another. Those of us who did not grow up to continue to be thieves are very lucky indeed. . . . By "lucky" I do not mean a play of fate, a felicitous concatenation of circumstances, a number of lucky breaks. What I mean by lucky is that that little boy was fortunate enough to be truly loved, fortunate enough to love in return, and therefore to sense the pangs of pain which both his father and his mother tried not to display. He was fortunate that his father recalled that he too had once been a thief when a little boy, and that his father did not permit his anxiety to become an overbearing, paternal, self-righteous hatred. That little boy, I repeat, was lucky, in that on the day of his first crime he was loved and was able to love in return, and his father was right when he said to himself, "He has committed his first crime. He has understood." [4]

Here Zilboorg emphasizes the fact that what is curative in the environmental management of the delinquent is not so much what is said and confessed, as what is *not* said and what *cannot* be confessed. Many sincere workers with maladjusted children are genuinely distressed to find that there is no open show of remorse on the part of the delinquent, no easy admission of guilt, seldom any tears of contrition. They seem to feel that their task would be more satisfying if only the child could be brought to a confession and then break down in sobbing remorse. What they fail to appreciate is that such a confession would be utterly worthless, at best mere histrionics. Nothing can be gained by persuading the delinquent to simulate emotions that are not his own. From his point of view a confession would be out of place, for on the unconscious level he had no choice but to steal in the hope that he would be able to find a way back to the person from whom, initially, he had full right to take what he wished – his mother. The child who steals is acting from an unconscious logic which he may sense but cannot verbalize. It is of little value to him to be told he has done something which the community regards as wrong. He knows it. To lecture him on his sinfulness or punish him severely will only turn his aggression on to the outside world and on to the moralist, and further delinquency is the likely outcome.

What *is* therapeutic is for him to sense the wrong he has done for himself, and to sense your pain in this. Then the positive process of self-curing may set in. 'One of the most valuable things which modern psychiatry has discovered is the presence of a conscience in every criminal, no matter how brutal the crime; the presence of a sense of guilt in every criminal, no matter how carefree and callous he may appear; and the presence of a sense of community interests, of group cohesiveness, no matter how anti-social he may appear.'[5] It is upon this innate conscience, not social strictures, that one has to depend in dealing with the delinquent, on this conscience and the child's increasing capacity to relate his own affectivity with reason and moral attitudes. When reason and feeling are not related to

---

4. *The Psychology of the Criminal Act and Punishment.* Tavistock, London, 1954, p.144.
5. ibid. p.128.

one another, the mere knowledge of right and wrong will not prevent anti-social behaviour.

If there is no apparent understanding in the anti-social child that he has caused inconvenience, loss or hurt to other people it is due to the early dissociation between aggression, instinctual love and reason which is so typical of the delinquent and near-delinquent adolescent. The most flagrant psychological fact in the vicissitudes of aggression is the flattening and dulling of the emotional tone of the individual. He may speak as if he understands "the nature and consequences of his acts", but if he does not feel it at all adequately he is like a man who is awake, normal, rational – but totally anæsthetic. Such a person is not a whole person. . . . The dulling of emotions, the failure to feel, has nothing to do with morality or immorality . . .[6] Where the emotions are dulled, the will cannot step in to control aggression because self-control can be effective only when reason and feeling work together. A full recognition of this fact would prevent much frustration and sense of futility on the part of those working with anti-social children and who are so often and so easily discouraged by the apparent emotional anæsthesia of the delinquent.

One distinguishing feature of the maladjusted child's reality sense is that he recognizes things and people in a purely perceptive way, without appropriate affectivity. This lends his behaviour a certain shrewdness which can be readily mistaken for a true knowledge of what he is doing, whereas even a casual examination reveals the almost puppet-show quality of his experiences. In his world human beings and things can have the value only of furniture. This is the point at which the maladjusted child's psychic reality approximates so nearly to that of the psychotic child.

It is futile for the worker in schools for maladjusted children to expect, at the outset at least, normal emotions and reactions. To demand that a child show emotions appropriate to the situation is to ask him to simulate that he is well. This he knows to be untrue. He needs to learn how to cry meaningfully and in the proper context.

If he can cry, if he can feel depressed, if he can encompass the array of emotions associated around the original experience of deprivation, then guilt becomes possible, self-punishment becomes possible, and restitution becomes possible. 'What the law fails to

6. ibid. p.71f.

see is the curative power of healthy self-punishment which never becomes hostility. And what the law further fails to see is that punishment alone inflicted from outside produces only a hostile response, an intensification of hatred, and consequently a diminution of those healthy, auto-punitive, restorative trends in man, which alone make man capable of inwardly accepting punishment and making salutary use of it.'[7]

Returning then to practical issues: it is clear that if the aim of the teacher, warden, or house-father is to persuade a child to confess what he has done, to admit that he knows right from wrong, and to show remorse, then all that will be achieved is that the child will become a liar as well as a thief. He will lie only to satisfy the anxieties of the adults because these are not his true feelings. He will also be schooled to lie to himself because the motives and emotions that belong to the unconscious drives have nothing to do with the act as seen externally by the community or the school staff.

It is important at this point to distinguish between an 'inflicted' and a 'personal' sense of guilt. The moralist or conscientious teacher who finds relief from his own anxieties in extracting a confession from the delinquent child and who feels that in doing so he has furthered the therapeutic process is deluding himself. He is only demanding that the child shall confess what he already knows – that he has offended against the normal expectations and standards of society. To attempt to make the child 'feel guilty' on this plane is to be in touch only with what I have termed 'inflicted guilt'.

The effect of wringing this kind of confession from a child is:

(a) a transitory acknowledgment on the part of the child of external moral values, which has no true therapeutic advantage, and
(b) a blurring of the psychic problem, which is to find a path by which the child can get in touch with his own primitive and personal sense of guilt which relates to infantile processes long repressed.

I have many times been faced with the situation of a patient who, following some delinquent act or other misdemeanour, has been subjected to a long and heated tirade by a teacher or house-parent. To this tiresome and meaningless experience he has reacted with extreme anger and hopelessness, thus making it infinitely

7. ibid. p.112.

more difficult for me to get in touch with the child's own assessment of what he has done and relate this to his initial infantile predicament. Clinically speaking, therefore, it is incumbent on the teaching and management staff not only to tolerate a very considerable degree of nuisance-behaviour on the part of the child, but also to refrain from extensive moral harangues to which most of these children have already been long and pointlessly exposed.

Unless this condition can in large measure be met all that will be achieved is the casting up of a smoke-screen between the child as he is now and his primitive predicament. He may as a result become a comfortable conformist, paying lip-service to the values thrust upon him, but he will never sense his own responsibility, nor get in touch with his need to make restitution. Neither will he ever be able to use positively, and weld into his personality, his natural aggressiveness. So long as he remains in the super-charged moralistic atmosphere with its external sanctions and security he may conform. His real predicament will be revealed only when he leaves this tenuous and artificial environment.

Winnicott has said that: '*the nuisance value of the anti-social child is an essential feature*, and is also, at its best, *a favourable feature* indicating again a potentiality for recovery of lost fusion of the libidinal and motility drives.' It can only be comforting and reassuring to those who work in this intricate field to know that when the anti-social child is making himself a nuisance to his environment he is, in fact, beginning to show confidence in this new environment and giving evidence of an unconscious urge towards self-cure and rehabilitation. The child has sensed a willingness on the part of the environment to tolerate his regression to more primitive states of dependence. This must imply that, just as he wishes the environment to act towards him as a new and better mother, so it will permit him to act towards the environment as a dependent infant or small child. The normal child lays claim on the mother by a mixture of stealing from her body, hurting her body and messing on her body.[8] In order that a positive fusion of love and aggression may be achieved all these elements will be re-enacted symbolically within the milieu of the school and towards the more significant members of the staff.

For this reason the therapeutically orientated school for maladjusted children can never be a neat, tidy, orderly place in which

8. Winnicott, D. W., *Collected Papers*. Tavistock, London, 1958, p.311.

children obey instantly, never answer back, never swear and treat property with the reverence society would wish. The infant is not normally a tidy, clean, undemanding creature. He has withdrawn moods, violently aggressive moods, and periods of intense instinctual excitement. But by being able to experience all these moods and emotions in relationship to one loved and loving external object that is constantly present, he gradually gets a sense of personal wholeness and permissiveness in which he feels confident that all his emotions can be yielded to without destruction of the external object and therefore without threat to himself. In time he learns that aggression causes pain to others, accepts certain limits for himself, and masters the complicated skill of self-control as a method of preserving good objects and good feelings about external and loved persons.

Unless the school for disturbed children can provide an environment in which the child can gain this degree of emotional freedom and control it cannot perform therapeutic work beyond a certain low standard. At Bredinghurst we have observed again and again that the regressed child will test out many times the capacity of the environment to withstand his aggressive and anti-social behaviour, at first in a quiet and minor key but with gradually increasing vigour rising to a crescendo of irritating behaviour. When it seems that the school and the individual workers can literally stand no more, this violent testing-out ceases and the child then tends to become depressed before he is able to climb back to a more settled and responsible mode.

It is as though we were watching a re-enactment of the child's biting on the breast; it bites with gradually increasing ferocity until the mother is on the very edge of having to withdraw the nipple and leave the child angry, hungry, and frustrated. Perhaps the child at the breast senses that there are limits to the pain the mother can bear and at some joint summit of intense feeling – excitement on the part of the child and pain on the part of the mother – there is a sudden unconscious understanding that beyond this point rejection *must* take place by the mother's withdrawal. But at this critical moment the child becomes aware of the mother's pain as well as the instinctual excitement in himself as two sides of the same event, objective and subjective.

At this moment possibly a real fusion takes place between aggressive libidinal drives and excited lively love, in a primitive person-to-person relationship. From this fusion may stem both confidence in the employment of the instincts and self-control as a method of object- and self-preservation. It may be that this is the primitive infantile orgastic experience in which subjective feelings of excitement and gratification meet in 'harmonious pain' in two persons at the same moment. The elaboration and distortion of this primitive experience into sado-masochistic defensive relationships plays a very big part in the psycho-pathology of the maladjusted child. But that is a topic we cannot pursue here.

This, 'diagrammatically' at least, is the conclusion to which I have been led in my observation of boys under treatment at Bredinghurst. If there is any truth in it, it implies that without a capacity and a willingness on the part of the staff to experience and tolerate an intense personal sense of pain in relationship to the delinquent no truly therapeutic work can be done. It is perhaps the awareness of this singular symbiosis with the individual child that makes the work so personally exhausting and results in some members of the staff resigning before they are faced individually with such a crisis. It explains, too, why it is that from time to time there is a tendency on the part of certain members of the staff to revert to more punitive and less exacting methods of management.

'In the hopeful moment,' writes Dr Winnicott, 'the child:

'Perceives a new setting that has some elements of reliability.
'Experience a drive that could be called object-seeking.
'Recognizes the fact that ruthlessness is about to become a feature and so
'Stirs up the immediate environment in an effort to make it alert to danger, and organized to tolerate nuisance.
'If the situation holds, the environment must be tested and re-tested in its capacity to stand aggression, to prevent or repair the destruction, to tolerate the nuisance, to recognize the positive element in the anti-social tendency, to provide and preserve the object that is to be sought and found.'[9]

These are heavy demands which the anti-social child makes on individuals who are not his real parents, but unless these demands are recognized and met only partial recovery is possible – if there is any recovery at all. When the environment leads the child to what Winnicott calls 'the hopeful moment' by implied promises of

9. ibid. p.314.

imaginative holding and then abandons him, the last state of the child must be worse than the first. Which is, perhaps, why so many children discharged from non-therapeutic schools for the maladjusted quickly fall into psychopathy – the mark of the hopeful child who has been cruelly disillusioned and has decided for a militant state of dissociated existence.

10

Psychotherapy and the Law

UNDER the Children and Young Persons Acts of 1933 and 1948 it is clearly laid down that magistrates must at all times exercise their powers in the best interests of the child. Long experience of the workings of the London juvenile courts gives us no reason to doubt that the bench aims to do exactly that. Nevertheless magistrates have to balance the best interests of the child with the best interests of the society against which the child has offended.

The magistrates have a singularly difficult task. They must decide on what course to take after only a brief hearing during which various reports may be read from schoolmasters, social workers, possibly the warden of the remand home, and psychiatrists. They are also willing to listen to what the parents and other rightfully interested persons may have to say in court. These reports may be conflicting and the impression the child makes in court may appear to belie any hopeful view expressed by those who have had long knowledge of him. In these adverse circumstances it is still incumbent on the magistrates to arrive at a decision which may fatefully affect the boy's whole future. Unfortunately, unlike those who have the day-to-day handling of the child, there is no easy way by which magistrates can follow through a case for some years in order to determine whether a decision made in court was a wise or a disastrous one. It is difficult for them to know the relative merits of all the remand homes, detention centres, approved schools, Borstals, and schools for maladjusted children to which a boy may be sent. Neither have they, as the social workers and therapists have, any first-hand knowledge of the child's home or of the personalities of his parents.

In addition, so long as our judicial system favours punitive and preventive measures as against prophylactic techniques the position of the psychiatrist will remain a difficult one in court. It is sometimes unavoidable that a magistrate will arrive at facile conclusions. Pleading in court for a boy from Bredinghurst to be returned to us, we stated that the offence for which he was being charged took place while he was at home on holiday. We explained that the boy's mother had told him that she intended to apply for a revocation of the Fit Person Order so that he could return home (a circumstance which the child dreaded) and that we considered this fact and certain other stresses in the home precipitated a state of acute anxiety in the child which resulted in his stealing. The chairman of the bench was quite unable to disguise his scorn for so obtuse a view of what he considered to be a straightforward case of larceny and, looking past us, said: 'But I can see two perfectly decent and reasonable parents sitting behind the lad!' What he did not know (although had he read the reports in front of him he should have known) was that the boy's mother had four children by three different men, that the boy had never known his real father, and that the mother had recently become engaged to a young man half her age who was bitterly resented by the boy himself. The man sitting beside her was not, as the magistrate chose to assume, the boy's father but the mother's brother who had only just been released from prison!

We do not wish to imply that all, or even many, magistrates approach the problem with quite the same bland self-assurance, but the incident does illustrate how easy a matter it is for a magistrate, pressed for time, to leap to false conclusions and arrive at decisions based upon subjective attitudes rather than on an informed and sympathetic view of what is in the best interests of the child.

A further severe complication is that very few magistrates have any training in child psychology, nor have they had experience of working in a therapeutic environment with children. It is greatly to the credit of the bench that in the vast majority of cases in which we have appeared the magistrates have obviously been relieved to find that the school and the psychotherapist have not only sent in reports but been willing to speak for the child in court. They usually return him to our care, indicating that they have some confidence in our capacity to estimate what course is likely to be the best one to pursue, and are content that we are willing to accept continued responsibility for the child.

There are two major difficulties which the school and the therapist have to face in court. The first is, as we have hinted, the lack of understanding in the magistrates of the unconscious drives which underlie delinquency. As Winnicott says: 'We even have magistrates who fail to see that thieves are unconsciously looking for something more important than bicycles and fountain pens.'[1] An unavoidable conflict exists between the law, which assumes simply that all stealing is wrong and deserving of punishment, and the therapist, who knows that delinquent episodes are virtually inevitable in the course of the treatment of a deprived child, and that when a severely repressed melancholic child can go out and steal it may be a sign of hope and a new liveliness in him. Indeed if a boy can go out and help himself to something from Woolworth's it may be the first sign that he believes he can make a claim for himself or dare hope that his environment will provide any good thing for him.

It is to the credit of many of the magistrates that they are capable of accepting this view of delinquency or at least are prepared to give grudging agreement to what we say as being possibly true, and to give the boy 'one more chance'. Fortunately, too, many boys have been given 'one more chance' several times over, even by the same magistrates! This genuine concern on the part of magistrates, and their general willingness to concede that we also have the boy's and society's best interests at heart, gives us good reason to hope that, though magistrates must continue to represent the law and society, they are reluctant to use their important office in ways that might baulk the child's ultimate chance of full recovery.

The second inevitable conflict between the law and the school arises from the fact that magistrates have no real option but to focus their attention on one very limited aspect of the child's behaviour. They never see the child unless he has first committed an offence, even if that offence is only that he has been so unmanageable at home that the parents have reached the conclusion that he is beyond control. Invariably when the therapist is called into court, he has to account for some act of delinquency on the part of a child he is treating.

It cannot be avoided, therefore, that the magistrate and the therapist view the child differently. The magistrate is involved with the child mainly as a threat to society: the therapist is interested in

1. *The Child and the Outside World.* Tavistock, London, 1958, p.236.

him as a whole human being whose delinquency is but a small part of the total pattern of emotional illness. It sometimes happens, therefore, that when a boy becomes delinquent while at Bredinghurst and the therapist and the headmaster state that we are confident of success, the magistrates are apt to question the grounds on which we make so optimistic a prediction.

In a recent case one of our boys was charged with forging his mother's signature, thereby obtaining a small sum of money. He had been at Bredinghurst and under treatment for three years. Before his admission to the school at the age of ten he had no convictions but came to us under a Fit Person Order. After a year he was charged with larceny but discharged unconditionally. A year later he stole a bicycle and this time was given a year's conditional discharge. Within a month of the termination of the discharge he committed the act of forgery with which he was now charged and which he freely admitted.

The headmaster's report stated that in many ways he had made good progress while at the school and he would be willing to have the boy back. I insisted that the boy had, from the psychiatric point of view, made real strides towards full recovery, that to interrupt treatment at this stage would probably prove disastrous, and that I was confident that, in time, he would be able to return home and take up work. Nevertheless I added that I did not consider the boy was yet fit to leave school, although he had reached school-leaving age, and wished him to stay at Bredinghurst for a further year.

The chairman of the bench clearly showed that she was disturbed by the fact that the longer the child had stayed in our care the more serious his delinquencies had become – 'this crescendo of crime', as she called it – and was inclined to send him to an approved school. I then pointed out that the court could do no other than take into account the delinquent acts and little else. They could not retrospectively see the boy as he was when admitted to the school. When he originally came to us he was apathetic, depressed, and completely withdrawn. Though twelve, he did not know how to play. When given a toy he would place it gently on the floor and look at it in complete silence. He never spoke above a whisper. Food had no interest for him; cake was no more appetizing than boiled potatoes. He ate little, lay awake for hours, at night, wetted and soiled himself by day and night, and had virtually no contact with either children or staff. If anyone called his name he would automatically raise one arm to shield his head as if expecting to be struck, as he had so often been by his sadistic foster-parents. His foster-mother, who was in fact his great-aunt, had told him nothing of the circumstances of his birth and allowed him to believe he was her own child. He was suspicious of everyone's motives, expected rejection and violence, did not believe he had any rights, and was quite unable to give or respond to affection. When I assured him that he could play with the toys in my room he was incredulous and thought that this was only a trick, and that I would snatch them away in order to hurt him. He never played games with other children, and had never done so in the past. He had no friends, no ties, no sense of belonging anywhere, and had parted from his parents when he was admitted to the school without any sign of emotion, as though he were merely an inanimate object being moved from there to here.

After some time in treatment he developed a deep attachment to me and would make touchingly sensitive gestures of affection. He would slip little inconsequential notes under my door, draw pictures for me, bring me cups of tea and stand patiently outside the clinic merely to pass the time of day. Sometimes he would stand or sit outside my window and sing quietly over and over again, 'Oh my papa, how wonderful you are to me,' or 'Softly, softly come to me and open up my heart.'

Bit by bit he grew confident enough of my concern and affection for him to permit himself to be increasingly aggressive and over a long period would viciously attack me or throw a fit of temper and then storm out, leaving the room in a complete shambles. He was no longer living in a world of unreality. He established meaningful relationships among other members of the staff, made firm friendships among his peers and was able to attend an ordinary day-school while still resident at Bredinghurst. His intelligence was not high and his academic work was retarded, but he joined the Cadet corps at school and left it, reasonably enough, because the drill bored him.

It was about a boy like this that the magistrate was able to say with a touch of scorn: 'Of course we are only lay people, but we find it hard to believe that there is any sign of progress.'

Magistrates in juvenile courts would not, one might suggest, be undermining justice if they were to accept that, when a headmaster or therapist asserts that a boy has made good progress, this opinion is based on an intimate knowledge of the child and an historic view of the case which the court cannot gain. As a result of the generalized suspicion of psycho-analytical methods in this country there is a discernible tendency on the part of some magistrates and probation officers to believe that the therapist is trying to find a way round the law for those boys who are in treatment. This is to some extent understandable since, had it not been for the fact that a boy was in treatment, he might well have been sent to an approved school. No therapist, however, can placidly accept a verdict of a court which takes such action as will terminate treatment at a time when he believes the outcome may still be successful. He has two cogent reasons: first, because he is convinced that it is in the boy's and society's best interests that treatment should be brought to a successful conclusion, secondly, because if any good work is being done the therapist must invest a phenomenal degree of personal concern and skill in each patient.

To remove a boy from treatment must, therefore, be felt by the therapist to be an experience that is personally depleting; several years of intense and devoted work may be negatived or destroyed by a decision hastily arrived at by magistrates who have neither the skill nor the time to understand just what an intricate piece of work they have terminated. The therapist will, at times, find all this deeply frustrating, since a magistrate cannot, of course, be called to account for the decisions he makes (except by senior justices). If he returns a boy to us it is we who continue to hold the responsibility and the magistrate will probably never see the child again. Only we know what advances and gains have been made. If he removes the child from our care and places him in an approved school, once more the magistrate does not have to answer for whatever may happen thereafter. If the boy gets into trouble again, which he very likely will, either he appears at a distant court and the original magistrates never hear of it (and even if they did, what is one case among so many?), or else the further acts of delinquency are only interpreted as confirmation that the original decision was the right one because 'this boy is obviously cut out for crime and further treatment would have been a waste of time. . . .' This could be a false conclusion.

In line with this conflict is the habit of juvenile courts, and particularly of clerks of the court, to make great play of asking boys: 'Did you know it was wrong to do this?' Invariably the boy does know what he did was, in the eyes of the law and society, wrong; and invariably he admits that he knows and knew at the time of the offence. This theme is then taken up against the therapist, the magistrate implying that the child cannot be seriously disturbed emotionally if he knew that his action was legally wrong.

As we pointed out in the last chapter, such an admission means nothing. Under our law as it stands the psychiatrist in the criminal court for adult offenders is compelled to speak to a definition of 'madness' which is not clinically acceptable. The rules on madness are framed on the notion that if a criminal knew at the time that what he was doing was wrong he could not be mad. This legalistic bias filters down into many juvenile courts where it is assumed that after the age of eight a child is responsible for his acts and has a developed moral sense which, unless he is 'bad', will hold him back from doing whatever may be unacceptable to society.

The therapist, by contrast, is aware that there is a marked dissociation in the delinquent child which allows him to act within a world of complete or partial unreality and to perform anti-social acts, knowing them to be 'wrong', but without the accompanying feeling-tone and sense of guilt which, in the normal child, holds him back from actual delinquency.

Further, the therapist knows that whereas the child in a good home can take a shilling from his mother's purse when he is feeling temporarily deprived of her love and have the situation dealt with in the home, the institutionalized child has to make a more dramatic gesture to say the same thing. His mother is not there to steal from and even if she were, he has long ago despaired that she would understand such a gesture as being a plea for love, and so he has to steal from outside the home. But this brings him immediately into conflict with the law and with a community which offers him no deep ties, affection, or responsibility. The deprived child has to act against society in hope, in situations where the more fortunate child acts against his mother in confidence.

Over and above this is the fact that the normal child in a healthy home is able to deal with many inner tensions, feelings of aggression and anxiety, by means of fantasy. The deprived child's fantasy life is severely inhibited and he may have no alternative but to turn anxiety into direct action against others. In the normal child there is a significant difference between fantasy and fact. In the deprived child fantasy *is* easily confused with fact. The normal child may think of stealing and know it to be wrong, so he does not steal. The deprived child steals first.

Many delinquent boys steal almost as though they were in a fugue, a half-dream state in which the sharp edges of reality have become blurred, and they wake up to an actual nightmare when the policeman lays his hand on them. Then they suddenly find themselves in the world of reality, forced to bear the consequences of an act which took place almost in fantasy. The act is performed in a state of mind in which the unconscious drives are uppermost and the child is seeking contact with a person (his mother). But he wakes to find that the consequences have to be answered for in a world in which all that is now seen by himself and the law is that he stole a pen which he didn't much want anyway.

It is necessary to distinguish between fantasy, which is the imaginative elaboration of primitive feelings and body experiences, and the facile fantasy of the delinquent that is superficial and betrays an incapacity for such an imaginative psychic elaboration. It is this superficial type of fantasy that the maladjusted and delinquent child carries, escapes into, and often acts out. Only through clinical handling and growing insight do these children become capable of enriching their relationships to reality and to people with subjective and affectively rich fantasy life.

Where the secure family setting has been threatened beyond a certain point or destroyed by real difficulties in the parents, the child has to wake prematurely from a subjective state of dependence and fantasy to a premature state of self-caretaking; this reduces the pain of the actual trauma but is achieved only at cost to the personality and by the false fusion of reality and fantasy into something which has elements of both but in which neither is healthily complete.

It may be said, then, that the delinquent child exists in a world which is neither fantasy nor fact. In certain moods he is nearer fact, in others nearer fantasy, but in neither mood is there the clearcut delineation which the normal person takes for granted. For the clerk of the court, therefore, to ask him: 'Did you know that what you were doing was wrong?' is for the child to listen to a question to which the only answer is 'Yes', but which is being asked by someone who exists in another dimension altogether and for whom right and wrong have a very different subjective connotation. There will always be a conflict between the administration of the law and the understanding of the child, between punishment and compassion, between legal rectitude and emotional illness.

It is vitally important that this should not be misunderstood. Nothing, in my view, is more damaging to the child nor to the hopes of real progress in this branch of medico-sociological work than a sentimental attitude towards the delinquent. It is a vital function of the law as represented by the juvenile court not only to protect society against the offender, but also to protect the criminal against the society's feelings of revenge. Every anti-social act, no matter by whom it is committed or against whom, cannot fail to add something to the accumulation of public vengeful feelings against the criminal which, if given full rein, would result in violence. This feeling against the offender, whether juvenile or adult, has to be recognized frankly as necessary in society and is the basis of a social conscience. In a cultured community we permit the law to act on our behalf against the criminal, thereby restoring the social sense of justice and emotional balance.

Merely to plead, as some do, that the juvenile delinquent should never be punished because he is ill and not, therefore, responsible for his acts is to run the risk of building up in the community at large too great a demand for vengeance which would eventually result in a complete revolt against the therapeutic approach and a return to harsher law. It is for this reason that, difficult as it may be for the psychiatrist and the psychotherapist, it is necessary and right that he should have no powers, other than those open to him as advocate, to influence the decisions of the magistrates. The worst possible solution would be for the psychiatrists to be given the power to make the ultimate decisions. Psychiatrists are not judges.

It is the judge and the magistrate on whom the responsibility rests to decide what degree of licence and tolerance the community can bear at any given moment. We hold no brief for the view that juveniles should be exonerated because they are unhappy children who have been more sinned against than sinning – true though this may sometimes be. Nor do we claim that, merely because we are willing to advance a good prognosis and to take continued responsibility for the child, the court should do as we ask. For the task of the therapist is not merely to investigage the mind of the delinquent and press back to original psychic conflicts. His task, ultimately, is to help the delinquent to fit himself for life in a specific community, without causing it undue hurt. And he can only do this so long as the community, its needs and its laws, are taken as part of the over-all setting with the law as the ultimate arbiter. Therapy cannot succeed in a vacuum. The psychotherapist cannot profitably go faster than the speed at which the community is willing and persuaded to follow. To attempt more by sentimental appeals for compassion for the deprived child, which might conceivably result in well-meaning but shallow legislation, would be to risk all that we have so far gained.

11

Theory and Practice

PROBABLY the most succinct statement on the psychic problem underlying maladjustment is that of Dr D. W. Winnicott in his paper, 'The Anti-social Tendency'.[1] In this chapter I wish to relate what Winnicott has to say on the anti-social child to the management problems of such children within the therapeutic environment.

The common denominator of maladjustment, the constantly present element in all these children, is an actual environmental failure in infancy, a real and specific deprivation at a pre-genital level. The maladjusted child has suffered the actual loss of something good and positive in the mother-child relationship. On a deep level of self-awareness he 'has reached to a capacity to perceive that the cause of the disaster lies in an environmental failure'. The positive element, therefore, which every maladjusted child brings to those who have to deal with him is that he compels the environment to be important on the path back to health just as it was the environmental failure that led to illness.

The first essential in the treatment of the maladjusted child is the provision of a new and emotionally healthier environment which will take over management. To attempt therapy without being able to place the child in such an environment presents the therapist with a near-impossible task in all but the simpler cases. It was a correct interpretation of the unconscious needs and demands of the maladjusted child that led our social services first to provide schools for emotionally disturbed children rather than merely to offer outpatient treatment while keeping the child in the very home which had failed him at a critical point in his development. Unfortunately these schools in the main have lacked the skill and necessary understanding to take the problem further, to recognize and allow

[1]. *Collected Papers.* Tavistock, London, 1958, p.306f.

for what this new environment must mean for the child. Stress has been laid on re-education to the exclusion of the need for permitted regression allied with psychotherapy, which alone can enable many of these children to integrate their personalities and then come forward again.

If constructive work is to be done the child will expect of his new environment that he be permitted to regress, in mood and in emotional demand, to the point at which the initial failure took place. If this cannot be done, whatever other gains result, the child must remain to a greater or lesser degree emotionally crippled. A reasonably permissive attitude on the part of the school is, as we have seen, an essential element in the cure. Since the initial failure took place at a pre-genital level it is inevitable that, given the requisite security and tolerance, the child will regress to oral and anal levels of development in all three aspects: libidinal, aggressive, and ego.

It is of paramount importance here to distinguish between the over-permissive environment which tacitly encourages regressive behaviour in the child, as though it were an end in itself, and the therapeutic environment which controls and permits regression consciously, with an acute awareness of what is taking place in the child and its implications both to the child himself and the adult setting. Regressive phenomena without this control and awareness may be no more than a meaningless excursion into the bizarre. In practical terms, however, allowances must be made for the maladjusted child who, on the path to health, will become less tidy, more aggressive verbally and/or physically, and whose social behaviour will revert at times to a stage more consistent with that of a child of two or three than that of an adolescent.

Everyone who has worked in a school of this kind has remarked upon the anal-aggressive language which these children use towards the various members of the staff, upon their aggressive use of nicknames among themselves, upon the constant complaints they make against the school and particularly about the quality of the food they are given, upon their non-acceptance of normal standards in hygiene and good manners. They mess with their food, refuse to eat or else eat greedily, may develop voracious appetites, or, like small children, get most excited and unmanageable at mealtimes.

Oral behaviour of this kind, along with swearing and outbursts of uncontrollable temper, are often regarded with distaste and disgust by adults who feel their duty lies in trying to teach these children good manners, adult standards of behaviour, and a proper regard for those who care for them. What is so often overlooked is that in adopting socially objectionable modes of behaviour the child may in fact be paying the highest compliment he can to the adults in whose care he finds himself. He is actually saying that he feels so attached to them and so secure in their understanding of him that he can behave towards them as though they were good parental figures who will bear with his untidiness and excited aggression as a good mother bears with similar behaviour in the infant.

Anal strains in childhood behaviour also offend a large percentage of child-care staff who feel that the youngster who soils himself, wets his bed or urinates in his bath is either doing so out of spite or has never been taught the rudiments of proper hygiene and self-control. There is a tendency, therefore, in some schools for adults to attack these regressive symptoms in the false conviction that their eradication is an earnest of cure.

Ten years ago the school staff at Bredinghurst used to talk about 'treating enuretics', and many boys were sent regularly to a 'wet-bed clinic' at a city hospital where they were given medication and amusing little cards with a square for each day of the month, each square to be marked 'W' or 'D' according to whether the child had been wet or dry! In recent years enuresis has very seldom been discussed, no attempt has been made to treat a child specifically for enuresis or soiling, these things being recognized as part of, and accepted as an essential element in, the child's total disturbance and claim on his environment which clear up alongside his general improvement.

The normal infant lays claim on his mother by a mixture of stealing from her, hurting and messing. If the therapeutic environment is to rescue the deprived child, the staff must be willing to accept that equivalent demands will be made by the child on the adults in the environment. There will be stealing, mostly in the school, just as the small child who is near-normal steals in the home. There will be aggressive, boisterous, and violent behaviour, at times directed against the staff, often to the point of real pain or anxiety. And, for a time, there will be messing, untidiness, vulgarity, and slovenliness.

The ultimate test of normality is the fusion of aggressivity with libido, and the ability in the ego to bear hate and love towards the same object. The child who develops normally in a good home feels secure enough to hate and love his mother, and so come to terms with the diverse elements in his own nature and feel at home in aggression as in affection. The maladjusted child has not this advantage. The therapeutic school exists to give him a second chance – a chance to fuse within his own personality anger and gentleness, excitement and passivity, violence and tenderness, love and hate.

If the child seizes this second chance an inner process is set in motion which carries him back affectively to that point in his infancy at which the original deprivation took place. In the regressed state he will make demands upon the school staff which are his equivalent of the demands the infant makes upon the mother. Just as the good-enough mother is able to tolerate the infant's aggression, messing and excitement, so the child-care staff must be willing to tolerate regressive phenomena in the older child. It is this quality of toleration that makes adult love convincing to the emotionally ill child and enables him to link this experience with the more positive elements in his early relationship with the mother. If all goes well he will recover the lost fusion of the libidinal and aggressive (or motility) drives.[2]

In the main, however, the therapist himself will inevitably assume the paramount parental role with the children who are under treatment, and it will be in the consulting-room that much of the violent behaviour will occur. Only in the transference relationship of the therapeutic setting can all the complexity of conflicts be worked through to the point of insight and integration. The therapist will be the object of the most intense affection and the most intense hatred, and on his shoulders will fall the heaviest responsibility for enabling the child to arrive at a stable understanding and resolution of his emotional disturbance.

In his introduction to Aichhorn's book, *Wayward Youth* (Putman, London, 1936), Freud wrote: 'The educator should be psychoanalytically trained; otherwise the child, the object of his effort, remains an inaccessible enigma to him. Such training is best achieved when the educator subjects himself to an analysis in order to experience it within himself. Theoretical teaching of analysis does not penetrate deeply enough and brings no conviction.' The enormous advantages which accrue to a school when the head-

2. ibid. p.311.

master or headmistress has had a personal analysis are amply demonstrated in the work of Aichhorn, Bettleheim, Dockar-Drysdale,[3] and others. An analytical training not only enables the teacher to understand something of the nature of the personality problems which the child presents, but also equips him and his co-workers to bear a quite astonishing degree of anxiety in the management of the school, and consequently bring about remarkable cures in extremely difficult and anti-social children. In his chapter on 'The Aggressive Group'[4] Aichhorn recounts how he himself took over the management of twelve boys who were so unruly that they could not be tolerated in any other group in the school.

He recognized that the strong hate reaction that each of these boys showed was covering up an intense feeling of rejection and loss of love. In contrast to the ordinary educators he realized that severe discipline would be valueless and that the first task was to compensate to these children for their lack of real love, and to accept, despite all signs to the contrary, that beneath their violent behaviour was an appeal to be allowed to find a path through to being able to love and make restitution towards loved objects.

Aichhorn decided to see what would happen if he permitted these boys to be as full of rage and destruction as they wished while continuing to be treated with kindness and consideration by the adults in charge. What did happen is now well known. 'It is easy,' wrote Aichhorn, 'to understand that aggression can rise only to a certain pitch. If we do not check its course, an explosion is inevitable. Since we did not oppose the destructive behaviour of this group, their aggression was bound to reach a climax. When this point came the aggression changed its character. The outbursts of rage against each other were no longer genuine, but were acted out for our benefit. I recall an incident of this period which had the appearance of being serious. One boy threatened another with a bread knife at his throat, yelling: "Cur, I'll cut your throat!" I stood by quietly, doing nothing and apparently taking no notice of the danger which seemed to threaten. It was clear that this was only a feigned attack and therefore not dangerous. Since I acted as if this were not unusual, our hero threw the knife on the floor in

---

3. See 'The Residential Treatment of "Frozen" Children', *The British Journal of Delinquency*. Vol. ix, number 2, 1958. Also *The Howard Journal*. Vol. x, number 2, 1959.

4. op.cit. p.167ff.

rage, stamped his feet furiously, and then let out an inarticulate howl which later turned into violent weeping and continued until he was exhausted and fell asleep. Similar scenes were enacted by each of the twelve. Our ignoring the aggression brought forth in each case violent emotion which spent itself in weeping and rage. These outbursts were followed by a period of emotional instability. . . . During this period an emotional bond between the boys and the workers began to develop. . . . The boys had become unusually sensitive and now gave evidence of rivalry and jealousy even greater in degree than we expect to find in the nursery. . . .[5] This period of instability was finally followed by acceptable and social behaviour.'

The problem which confronts us is: how can a school which is run by non-analytically trained staff be expected to bear this high level of anxiety? Fortunately if a school is well established the staff will never be presented with a group of twelve boys acting in this disconcerting manner all at once, but only with one or two boys at a time reaching this pitch of violent and angry behaviour. It is the task of the therapist not only to support the teaching and housestaff when a child is behaving aggressively, to help the other workers to understand what is happening and so keep the episode in perspective, but also to bear the brunt of the major assault himself.

It is seldom long before a boy feels the need to make physical contact with the therapist, as though he were testing out his 'thereness'.[6] Usually this takes place first in an affectionate or play context. A boy may creep up behind me in the playground and quietly slip his hand into mine without a word, or he may jump on my back, or rush into my room and slap me boisterously on the back and yell cheerfully: 'Hullo, Doc!'

> Tim, a severely depressed child, gradually showed signs of increasing excitement during his analytical hours. He would give exciting extracts from films he had seen or incidents he had observed and gesticulate generously with his hands, gradually coming nearer and nearer to me. During one of these exciting monologues he accidentally cut the back of my hand with one of his fingernails and, though the scratch was minute, a few drops

5. ibid. p.175f.
6. cf. Mahler, M. S., and Furer, M., 'The Symbiotic Syndrome of Infantile Psychosis'. *Psychoanalytic Quarterly*, xxix, p.317–327.

of blood seeped from the cut. In a flash Tim ran from the room and for a few minutes I could not find him. I began to mount the stairs to look for him. He heard me coming and when I reached the top of the flight I saw him flinging himself in panic against a locked door, like a sparrow trapped in a greenhouse.

I called out, reassuring him that he had not killed me and that in fact I was scarcely hurt. He looked at me as though I were a ghost and flung himself on the floor at my feet, sobbing and begging forgiveness. For a long time he sat at the head of the stairs weeping inconsolably and moaning: 'Whenever I get excited, something dreadful happens.'

I mention this incident not only to show the varied ways in which children test out the willingness of their new environment to tolerate their physical presence and its capacity to bear normal, spontaneous childlike contact, but also to illustrate the admixture of hope and dread, of wishing to be tolerated and fear of being rejected, which may lie behind an apparently simple act of reaching out towards a loved object. Not a few maladjusted children harbour an inner terror that in establishing contact with an adult for whom they have a lively affection they will damage or destroy the person concerned.

Gradually these physical contacts become more aggressive. The aggressive element is first introduced at some point where the child feels the therapist has acted in a hostile manner. Very frequently this occurs during the first interview of a new term when the boy is resentful of the break in the transference relationship, or after the therapist has been ill (and again, from the patient's point of view, been rejective) or following an interpretation which sets up acute panic:

Tim, for example, some time after the scratching incident, spent much of his time swearing at me for my supposed ill-treatment of him. On one occasion he sat with his back towards me pouring out a torrent of vitriolic accusations. I didn't see him just when he wanted. . . . I was a liar, a quack, a confidence trickster. . . . I only pretended to be fond of him so that he would tell me of his delinquencies and then I would betray him. . . . I was ugly, a bastard, a cunning bugger, and much else. He then fell silent and, as I began to interpret his mood and material and link it with his childhood experiences, I noticed his hands slip down and grip the sides of his chair. With a sudden lithe and agile movement he slid off the seat of the chair, twisted round and stood up with the chair now poised above his head. He brought it down with all his force on me. Fortunately I was not unprepared and was able to parry the blow. The chair fell to the floor and Tim sat himself heavily beside it, with his back to me again and his head in his hands. Suddenly he was convulsed with sobs, deep, violent, comfortless weeping. Slowly he composed himself and after a time went to the desk, took out a piece of paper and drew a picture of Humpty-Dumpty lying on the ground after having fallen from the wall, and all in pieces.

The question why the maladjusted child can come to know his feelings first only through behavioural and actual contact is one which is of paramount importance in the understanding of this problem and in the next chapter I shall discuss it further.

Once a child has established by actual experiment that aggressive behaviour neither destroys the therapist nor threatens the transference relationship his angry outbursts may reach a crescendo of rage. Usually at this stage there occurs a climax of violent feeling in which the boy may not only attack me but try to wreck my room. It is vitally important over this period not to react to aggression with aggression but to preserve sufficient detachment as to be able to make interpretations and at the same time prevent the child from doing himself, myself, or the school property too much harm. Often the child will storm out of the room, slamming the door with the utmost force. In these circumstances I merely open the door again and sit down and wait. On the first few occasions the boy will probably not come back, but go over to his classroom in a furious temper or, perhaps, run away. After a time, however, he comes back into my room following such a bout of fury, usually in a calmer mood. It is not too difficult to bear the hurt and anxiety which these attacks produce so long as the child does not use a weapon. Fortunately in my experience it seems that at the actual crisis of rage a child finds greater satisfaction in using his fists directly on the hated person, and once he begins to use a weapon it is generally a sign that we have moved into the stage, also noted by Aichhorn, in which there is an element of acting.

I have often had a knife held at my throat by a boy who appears determined on murder. Many times I have had chairs thrown at me or been threatened with iron bars, baulks of wood, scissors, and home-made stilettos. It is very important in these circumstances to let the child feel that one is not afraid and will not allow his agression to get out of hand. When one has observed many times that knives thrown in fury have a habit of just missing, that bricks always fall short and chairs fly through the air just to one side, one becomes accustomed to the notion that actual murder is not intended.

My experience bears out that of Aichhorn, for most of these attacks are followed by a violent outburst of emotion, weeping and loss of control. Only twice have I actually had to protect myself out of fear that a boy might cause me serious injury. In both these cases there was a sudden upsurge of feeling on the part of the child following an interpretation I had given him. In both cases the boys slowly recovered from the outburst as though they were waking from a bad dream and were enormously reassured to find that they had done me no major injury.

It has been asked whether it is possible for a woman analyst to treat the really anti-social and violent adolescent boy. Personally I doubt it. A boy of thirteen or fourteen, well-built and muscular, is aware that a woman could not easily withstand a flurry of violent blows, nor be able to protect herself if attacked with a knife. He knows unconsciously that the therapist's survival is vital to him and if she is unable to protect herself he must do the protecting. This means that he has to keep his rage rigidly under control in order preserve the therapist, and treatment must, then, stop somewhere short of abandonment. Besides few women would be able to stand, in the normal course of a day's work, heavy punches from the fists of strong young adolescents even when these punches are delivered in a friendly, affectionate, or merely excited mood. I am not implying here that therapy is a muscular exercise. But the fact remains that the majority of anti-social boys use their musculature to express affection and aggression, and a therapist needs to be able to absorb a good deal of punishment however lovingly meant.

The therapist is not by any means the only member of the staff who will meet with physical violence whether in a mood of excited affection or in hatred. Every member of the staff who has anything valuable to offer these children will at some time or other be either playfully or aggressively attacked. But since the therapist, by the very nature of his transference relationship with the patient, is the central figure in the child's psychic constellation, the actual crisis is likely to take place in the consulting-room.

I do not wish to give the impression that all maladjusted boys become violent and verbally or physically aggressive in the course of treatment. But very many do. Schools which demand consistent good behaviour from the boy and refuse to tolerate aggression do not offer him any reason for hope in his environment. Such a school may contain and manage disturbed children; it will not cure them. They may conform so long as they are in the school but at a later date they will act unsociably towards another environment (usually society at large), and become delinquent, thereby replacing the lost school control-management by a similar external control-management – the prison. The notion that by keeping a child long enough under discipline and instrucing him in moral precepts will make him accept both precepts and discipline as his own has no basis in fact and is not born out by the evidence. There is too much hatred and disillusionment in these children for them to accept what is offered. Without an opportunity to reach back into the past and experience again the unresolved tensions and conflicts of a disturbed childhood there can be no solution which does not somewhere involve the permanent distortion of the personality.

It has been remarked again and again by all the workers at Bredinghurst that the boys who have caused us the most trouble at one time or another seem so often to have turned out the best in the end. This general observation in itself supports our contention that only by being able to inflict pain on loved objects without producing an aggressive, rejective reaction does a child really get in touch with his own innate capacity to love, to make restitution, and to accept full responsibility for his own life.

Some mention should be made in this context of the withdrawn states to be noticed in the maladjusted child. In the normal home a child may withdraw into himself in a variety of moods, but does so within a setting which is particularly sensitive to his needs and which recognizes at all times his dependence. The mother's affection and her understanding of this need ensure that the child's withdrawal is observed and his mood met by a sensitive holding on by the parents.

The institutionalized child, to achieve the same effect, has no option but to make a more obvious gesture. If he were merely to become withdrawn in the fashion of the child in an ordinary home little notice would be taken of him. Besides, the sheer mechanics are more difficult in a school or institution. There is comparatively little privacy, he has no room of his own to which he can retire, and well-meaning teachers, school friends, and house-staff feel some compulsion to 'drag the child out of himself'. The child, on the other hand, wishes above everything at these times to be allowed to keep in touch with himself. Hence to gain privacy or the attention he craves he must make a greater demonstration than the normal child. Thus the institutionalized child will run away, or climb to the top of a tree and stay there for hours at a time, or sit in a cellar or on a roof at times when a normal child would merely retire to his bedroom or curl up in an armchair.

This momentary detachment from a waking relationship with external reality may have one of three meanings for the child: first, he may withdraw in a mood of sullen hostility towards his environment, feeling hurt, offended, misunderstood or himself enveloped in a mood of hate or defiance. Secondly, he may withdraw in order to keep in touch with meaningful or loved objects who are absent or, he fears, 'lost':

> During the war years Richard had been evacuated to the country when still a baby. From the age of one year until he was five he had been cared for by a kindly woman in Norfolk who had a young family of her own. Since his real mother never visited him and his father was in the Services Richard came to think of this woman as his mother and this family as his own. When the war ended the foster-parents wished to adopt him but his parents reclaimed him and he was taken back to London. By now there was a younger child in the home and Richard felt himself a stranger in the new environment.
>
> He never settled down with his parents and other siblings. He became persistently enuretic and encopretic. He was never known to smile and seemed to pass each day in a state of withdrawn apathy. He made no friends at school and little educational progress. His soiling and smearing infuriated the parents, particularly the

father who would beat him unmercifully or throw him in a cold bath when he messed his clothes.

For many weeks after his admission to Bredinghurst he made no contact with other children or staff and would wander around the grounds, hugging the hedges and looking downcast and miserable. I was able to discover that he spent virtually every moment of his waking day thinking about what he called 'my family', by which he meant the family in Norfolk with whom he had been billeted. His mother had not allowed him to keep in touch with these people and, when they wrote to him or sent him presents, she would burn the letters and give the presents to other members of the family as gifts from herself. Yet these early parental figures were the only people for whom Richard had any feeling, and the only way in which he could keep in touch with them was in his mind. In his withdrawn mood he was keeping alive every precious memory he had of them, telling himself stories about what they would be doing and, last thing at night, would conjure up a mental picture of his foster-mother kissing him and saying good night. Any attachment towards other people, any exciting event in the school he felt as a threat to this mental process, lest forgetting them for a moment might be an act of disloyalty or magically result in their death.

From one angle he was in a state of perpetual mourning, from another he was omnipotently keeping them alive. Our psychiatric social worker was able to persuade the mother to let us contact the family in Norfolk and Richard began a regular correspondence with them. He ceased to be encopretic, began to make progress in school and establish meaningful friendships with other children.

After he had been in the school about a year he suddenly reverted to his previous withdrawn state and would be found sitting alone in a corner of the field staring into space or weeping quietly. Eventually he was able to tell me that he had read in the newspapers that there had been serious flooding in Norfolk and this, combined with the fact that he had not had a letter from his onetime foster-parents for more than three weeks, had convinced him that they were all drowned. It was only after we were able to contact this family again and assure Richard that they were alive and well that he recovered from his mood of depressed withdrawal.

Thirdly, withdrawal may also be the child's way of keeping in touch with unconscious inward psychic processes, and be attempts towards integration which are so vague and unformed as to demand emotional isolation and privacy. Here the role of the therapist is of paramount importance for only he can help the child personalize these processes and relate them to the transference situation.

Dr D. W. Winnicott, in discussing withdrawn states, relates them to the patient's management in infancy. He writes: 'I would say that *in the withdrawn state a patient is holding the self* and that if immediately the withdrawn state appears *the analyst can hold the patient,* then what would otherwise have been a withdrawal state becomes a regression. The advantage of a *regression* is that it carries with it the opportunity for correction of inadequate adaptation-to-need in the past history of the patient, that is to say, in the patient's infancy management. By contrast the *withdrawn* state is not profitable and when a patient recovers from a withdrawn state he or she is not changed.'[7]

This statement points-up one vital contrast between the therapeutic type of school, which gives credence to the moods and unconscious conflicts in the child, and the merely educative type of school which aims to distract the child from unconscious inward moods and fantasies which, from time to time, prevent him from responding to normal social demands and reality situations.

Practically, this underlines the need for the school environment to be able to distinguish between the withdrawn state proper and the withdrawal as an aggressive technique of revolt. In both cases the child may run away from school, but the aim in each is different. It may perhaps be reasonable to punish the aggressive absconder, but to punish or upbraid the child who withdraws in depression or in order to keep in touch with an inward personal process is both unjust and profitless.

---

7. *Collected Papers*. Tavistock, London, 1958, p.261.

12

Clinical Observations

THE observations in this chapter refer only to the more disturbed type of child, the delinquent, and the severely maladjusted. They do not apply to the neurotic child whose treatment often follows a slow and regular graph of improvement. With the delinquent we have found it possible to enumerate six stages, more or less clearly defined, during the period of the child's stay in the school.

(1) *A comparatively brief period of benign behaviour.*

This may last only a few days or could be prolonged into several months.

Over this period the child will be relatively docile, obedient, conforming and helpful, so much so that one sometimes wonders what has happened to the child who was referred to us as 'impossible' or 'agressive, sullen, cunning and depraved'. This period of minimal friction is so constant a factor that it has become known among the staff as 'the honeymoon period'.

Inexperienced staff are easily deceived by this period of artificial benignity on the part of the child into believing that his mere placement in their school has brought about a miraculous and permanent change. Any subsequent defection would then be attributed not to the child's inherent personality distortions but to the supposedly corrupting influence of the less regenerate children in the school.

By constant encouragement and reassurance it is possible to prolong this period considerably. The child, having seduced the staff into false hopes, perpetuates the subterfuge by a façade of bland and compliant behaviour, by making rapid progress at his lessons, and generally giving the impression of normalcy. Of course fairly soon he reaches the ceiling of superficial improvement, but by now both he and the staff have invested their hopes in his capacity to maintain his false-self personality, and no attempt is made nor opportunity given for a thoroughgoing investigation into the nature and extent of his real predicament. In schools where the staff are open to this kind of deception glowing reports on the child's improvement and claims for rapid-cure methods are made which inspectors read with delight. Unfortunately one finds that these 'cures' have the unhappy knack of turning up a year or two later in approved schools or Borstals.

From the child's point of view this benign phase may serve a useful purpose, particularly if he is determined to find a path through to health. On admittance he has no knowledge of the staff, no way of knowing what are their capacities, how deep is their understanding, how sincere their regard. It is important to remember that, just as the staff are observing the boy and trying to assess the nature of the problem he will present to them, so the boy himself, quite legitimately, is observing the staff and attempting to weigh up exactly what they have to offer him. Over this period, he is an observer rather than an actor. He is carefully testing out the ground, seeking to establish the exact nature of the new environment in which he finds himself. For some considerable time he has no method of assuring himself that he can permit the staff to know just how disturbed he is.

(2) *The next stage is a period in which his symptoms become manifest.*

Provided the staff have the capacity to wait and observe, and do not leap in with active rescuing techniques, yet at the same time provide evidence of their willingness and ability to hold the child through a disturbing phase, he will gradually reveal the true nature of his illness. Through his gestural behaviour he will reveal his deeper anxieties, his tenuous grasp of reality, his aggressive or sadistic propensities, or his sense of inward disintegration.

Now the staff begin to realize why the boy was admitted and have an opportunity to assess to what kinds of strain and anxiety he will subject them before one can hope for cure. It sometimes happens that this stage is reached only after a child has been in treatment for some considerable time, for it may well be that his defensive organization is so rigidly established that only analytical probing will compel him to face his real predicament. Contrariwise we have sometimes found it best not to initiate treatment until this second stage is reached, choosing to interpret the child's gestural behaviour as an appeal for more specialized help. Occasionally this approach has had the fortunate result that psychotherapy has had to be given only over a very brief period.

Chris, for example, was in treatment with me for only three months, yet this period was critical and brought about profound changes. He had been at the school for eighteen months and during this time had made reasonably good educational progress. He was little trouble in the cottage, largely keeping himself to himself, though it was known that he did a good deal of pilfering, chiefly from other boys. He was good at games and generally gave the impression of a cheerful and ambitious boy. His cottage-father, who was an exceptionally sensitive man, many times mentioned in conference that there was a remarkable detachment about Chris. Everything he did was done without personal involvement, without feeling, and all his relationships with others were superficial and totally lacking in warmth or conviction.

In recent weeks, however, Chris had repeatedly asked me if I would find a place for him among the boys being treated and finally twice-a-week sessions were arranged. Over the first month or so he brought me literally hundreds of drawings of railway engines which he did in his spare time. All of these, he said, were Russian engines and he assured me that there was only one admirable country in the world, Russia. He wished he had been born a Russian and intended as soon as he was old enough to disappear behind the Iron Curtain. According to him the Russians were matter-of-fact-people who knew that love didn't mean anything, that all men were bastards at heart and relied solely on power and cunning, with the result that they were never deceived nor outwitted. He said he never dreamed, never fantasied, never had 'weak-minded things' like nightmares. He was tough, well armoured, and intended to see that whatever happened in life *he* would be all right.

I cannot here go into the clinical use I made of this material except to say that his obsession with railway engines had a threefold significance. They represented for him power without feeling (this aspect was reinforced by his conception of the Russian nature); dimly remembered happy days he spent when only three years of age wandering around Euston station with his father who now had remarried and showed no interest in the boy, and an account of a train disaster in which many people had been killed, a newspaper report of which he carried in his wallet, though I did not know this at the time.

During his fifth week in treatment he brought me yet another drawing of a railway engine which looked as though the bogey-wheels were coming off the lines. I suggested that his preoccupation with engines had to do with his fear that he might 'come off the lines', too, and be unable any longer to sustain his notion of himself as the iron man. It was at this point that he drew from his wallet the newspaper cutting I have mentioned, and admitted that he had been suffering from a deep but unformed sense of foreboding during the last few days. Then with a sudden and completely atypical sigh he said: 'I couldn't sleep last night.' He went on to say that since coming to see me he had been sleeping very badly because just as he was falling asleep he would see his mother, who died when he was four, standing at the foot of his bed. This apparition so terrified him that he would keep himself awake till dawn. He was able to recall many memories of her which had long been repressed. He described her features, her colouring, and then, with a start of surprise, he remembered that her christian name had been Margaret. Snatching a sheet of paper from the desk he attempted to draw her face, his eyes filled with tears.

Throughout the rest of the session he wept silently but managed to tell me that he was sent away to live with an aunt during his mother's last illness, that no one told him when she died though he knew she was desperately ill because he had seen her in hospital before going to his aunt's home in Devon. When he returned home a month later it was to a home without a mother. He was not convinced then and had not been since that she had in fact died. He believed that she had only been kidnapped and was being held prisoner somewhere. His father had never taken him to see her grave and even if he did he would not believe it was his mother buried there. People were capable of going to any lengths to deceive a child and could easily put up a gravestone with her name on it just to make him believe she was dead. At the end of the session he asked me for the address of Somerset House so that he could go there and find out for himself whether or not his father (who had since remarried) was a bigamist or not. One of the reasons why his behaviour at home had been so deplorable – at last his stepmother had issued an ultimatum that either Chris must leave or she would –

was that she was deeply involved in this conspiracy about his mother's 'death'. For years he had been in the habit of searching the face of every woman he met in the street and asking himself: 'Could *she* be my mother?'

During the next week Chris's cottage-father reported that the boy had been in a most disturbed state, weeping a great deal and complaining that he felt unreal, as though his limbs were detached from his body 'and all trembling inside'. He had slept little but, when he did, he woke terrified from a nightmare. He had also bought himself a crucifix which he tied round his neck to protect him from ghosts.

Chris reported these things to me also, saying that in his nightmares he had repeatedly dreamt that he was about to die or be killed, and he asked many questions about death. He felt that had he not gone to stay with his aunt at the time of his mother's last illness he might have prevented her from dying. For the first time he was willing to concede that she had died. By going away from home he must have been in some sense the murderer of his own mother and thus himself deserving of death.

The pictures he drew at this time were confused scribbles covering the whole of the page. Half-revealed among the tortuous lines were figures of ghosts, gravestones, men lying in coffins, female spirits sitting on their own graves, and crucifixes. He also raised the question of suicide and wondered if many so-called accidents were in fact unconscious suicidal acts.

I arranged to see him again the next day, and he arrived in a furious mood. He stalked up and down my room swearing at me, accusing me of being a liar, an ignoramus, bad like the rest. 'I would like to kick your fire in,' he said and did in fact kick at the gas-fire. 'Why my *fire*?' I asked. 'All right then,' he yelled, 'I'd like to kick your fucking teeth in!' His whole body was trembling as he went on to say what cruel and vicious things he would like to do to me, ending up: 'and cut out your guts and smear them all over the bleeding wall.' He clenched his fists so that the nails cut into the flesh and he bit the back of his hand till the blood began to flow. By now he was trembling so much that he had to sit down.

In the course of this tirade he accused: 'You're a bloody bugger, Dad. You don't deserve to live.' I now picked up this use of the word 'Dad' and began to make an interpretation along œdipal lines, but he would not listen. Pulling up his trouser leg he drew a long sheath knife from his stocking and leapt at me holding the knife against my chest. His face contorted with fury, he shouted: 'I've only got to push this one inch further and you're dead. I'd like to kill you and every other bloody bastard. I'm going to kill you anyway, for a start.' Facetiously, I reminded him that a condemned man was allowed to smoke one last cigarette and asked if he would permit me this indulgence. This infuriated him further, but he agreed. Then he turned the knife against himself pressing the point into his shirt. Finally he flung it at the door with such force that it dug into the wood.

Suddenly all the fight went out of him and he slipped to the floor sobbing loudly and uncontrollably. After a time he told me how tempted he was to take his own life, how in the last few days while eating his lunch he had had to hold his right hand with his left when using his knife, for fear he would plunge it into his heart, how he had had to run away from a bus in the street because he was aware of an impulse to thrown himself under it.

Towards the end of this long session lasting nearly three hours, he said: 'I've never talked to anyone like this before. I've never been so far before. It's all been terribly frightening, but I'm glad now I told you everything I felt. . . . Why aren't you afraid of me? I've never met anyone like you before. Why don't you get mad with me? I could have killed you, you know.' He then went on to say how frightened he was of going back to school in case he should 'accidentally' kill himself, and I offered to ask the headmaster if he could stay in bed or in the cottage for the rest of the day. This offer he declined on the grounds that if he was going to commit suicide he could do it just as well in the cottage as elsewhere.

Following this session, some of the significance of which I shall pick up in my next chapter, I saw Chris four times a week till the end of the term. Over this period we discussed more conventional analytical material of an oral, anal, and œdipal nature. From this time on the boy's behaviour and affective life changed dramatically both in school and at home, and he has gone on to make a sound adjustment to life generally.

It is clear, however, that without both good management in the cottage and psychotherapy it would not have been possible for the staff to discover exactly how ill Chris was, nor to see him through a crisis of this kind and at the same time give him real insight into his own inner predicament. He would have continued to remain an affect-deficient personality and would almost certainly either have become an inveterate delinquent or have committed suicide.

(3) *Next comes a period of playful physical contact.*
At the outset of residential treatment the delinquent child does not generally do much to seek the company of adults. He prefers to keep them at arm's length both psychically and physically. Once he has established confidence in the environment, however, and a thoroughgoing transference relationship has been set up, he will exploit every opportunity for playful physical contact with a well-liked teacher or house-parent and also with the therapist.

Uusually this takes place initially in a mood of exceptional excitement or a sudden upsurge of affection. Though delicately tentative at the outset, as though fearing rebuff, it gradually becomes more and more boisterous, the child throwing his whole excited musculature into violent contact with the adult. This 'physical mood' of excitement is most reminiscent of the infant's delighted and energetic play with his parents and the obvious pleasure the very small child gains from being thrown up in the air by a strong father or lovingly but roughly fondled by his mother.

There is a gradual crescendo in this playfulness, a greater degree of real aggression becoming more and more apparent. Alongside the mounting physical violence, oral forms of aggression creep in until the adult is being roundly abused, though still with an affectionate inflection in the voice and manner, in terms which include all the more coarse elements in the English language.

(4) *One can expect then a brief period of aggressive and irresponsible behaviour.*
Our experience would seem to indicate that on the path to cure the delinquent child has no alternative but to pass through a phase of violent or completely disorganized behaviour in which the environment takes over one hundred per cent responsibility. This crisis, fortunately of short duration, may occur either in the consulting-room, where social repercussions are nil, or in a brief spate of overt delinquency or maniacal loss of control in the cottage, the one common factor being that the transference-significant adult must bear the brunt of the aggressive or anti-social behaviour. One

of the administratively fortunate consequences of having psychotherapy integrated within the school is that the children in treatment are most likely to confine the peak of their most disturbed behaviour to the consulting-room, thereby reducing the toll upon the school and the local community. Should this climax take the form of delinquent or anti-social behaviour outside the clinical setting it is vitally important for the child to be absolutely certain that the headmaster and the therapist will support him throughout, will not threaten to dismiss him from the school or from treatment, and will give him opportunities afterwards to make adequate restitution.

It has been our unvarying experience that the child who has the courage to let go his controls in this way and depend solely for a time upon the sincerity, strength, and good offices of the, to him, significant members of the staff emerges from this disorganized phase with a very different personality structure, different affective reactions, and a greater capacity to use his energies and imagination constructively. It is as though inner psychic forces which had till now been wasting their effort in mutually inhibiting conflict were suddenly released and thus free to be applied in new and more fruitful directions.

I must, however, emphasize that over this phase the holding environment must show no signs of weakness, sentimentality or anxiety, otherwise the child has to take over the role of protecting the environment for, above everything else, he depends upon its continued existence.

Jack, a strong muscular boy of thirteen, used a novel method to show me just how much he depended upon my physique to give him this opportunity for maniacal release, without his having to be anxious about my capacity to survive. For some weeks he had been becoming more aggressive in his attitude to me, though always finding excuses for making it look as though his boisterous behaviour was mere hearty fun. When he came into my room he would slap me on the back with all the force at his command. Whatever comment or interpretation I made he would take as a faint insult and stand beside me feigning offence and striking me on the shoulder with his fist, keeping my arm well bruised for days at a time.

One day he reported that he had dreamt he was a knight jousting.

His opponent was a much smaller knight dressed in black armour with his visor down. At the first clash he drove his spear into the stomach of the smaller knight, knocking him from his horse and killing him instantly. He dismounted and strode up to the recumbent figure of the black knight and opened his visor to see who his opponent had been. He could not now recall seeing the face of his dead adversary in the dream but knew that he had been profoundly shocked and had woken up trembling and sweating with dread at what he had done.

Many interpretations were open to me, but for reasons which are too detailed to go into here I chose to say that I could tell him that the face on which he looked in the dream was that of his younger brother. At this Jack's face went suddenly pale, his lips tightened, and he made as though to put his hands around my throat and strangle me. With obvious difficulty he controlled this impulse and, turning to the desk, snatched a piece of paper on which he wrote:

'DECLARATION OF WAR.

'I, Jack R. L., hereby declare war on that fucking swine Dr Shields on this day 23 June 1959, and we shall fight to the death until I am forced into submission.

'(Signed), Jack R.L.'

This sheet of paper he thrust into my hands and scarcely gave me time to read it before he flung himself at me scratching, biting, and attempting to strangle me. With a boy so strong and agile it took all my strength to control him without injuring him.

In the two following sessions he made similar but less vicious physical attacks, at the same time covering me with foul abuse. Over this period he was a persistent nuisance in the cottage also and on one occasion ran away. On his return he was quieter, depressed, and prepared to listen to what I had to say without any show of violence or hatred.

The phrase in Jack's Declaration of War, 'we shall fight to the death until *I* am forced into submission' neatly condenses the delinquent's needs over this critical phase. He needs (a) to be able to channel all his aggression (uninhibited by fears of the other's capacity to survive) on to the loved (and hated) adult; and he needs (b) to know that he cannot destroy the loved object, that when the 'fight to the death is over' the therapist will still be there, uninjured, the victor who has held his position against the utmost fury of the child.

I would go so far as to hazard the opinion that, unless the treatment of the truly delinquent child can be brought to this pitch and the crisis seen through to its conclusion, whatever improvement may take place in the child it will be somewhat short of complete resolution. Once a child has experienced this type of affective climax and been able, later, to gain insight into what took place I have invariably felt he could be discharged from the school without my ever having to fear that he would become delinquent again. I have not so far been proved wrong in this.

(5) *There is then likely to be a period of marked depression or disorientation.*

Perhaps the most remarkable experience for the therapist who treats delinquent children is the astonishing change in mood and manner between the period of excited physical aggressiveness, which leads up to the maniacal climax, and the period of quiet sadness and 'lostness' which follows it. Other clinicians might feel that this would be a golden opportunity for detailed interpretations and retrospective working-through of the rich and dramatic material of the past weeks. Personally I have never felt this to be appropriate or likely to be rewarding. To me it seems that for a week or possibly a fortnight the child needs to find in me a relaxed and affectively unagitated mood in which I can respond to him if need be, but in the main simply be there in a holding role. Sometimes a child will merely greet me in an affectionate fashion and then sit silent for the rest of the hour on the rug by the fire, occasionally looking up to smile at me. Other boys might choose in this period to find excuses for touching me in a fondling fashion as though reassuring themselves that I am uninjured and assuring me of their basic affection.

Without exception, however, the time comes when they themselves wish to discuss their own feelings and reactions to what has taken place, to talk about their present puzzlement at their depressive moods and feelings of disorientation. More often than not they will use such a phrase as: 'everything looks so different these days. I can't make it out.' I feel that once this mood has arrived we are on the last stage of treatment.

(6) *Finally a period of working through and reorientation.*

In the months of analytical work preceding this climax the

therapist has to use classical techniques and interpretations on the oral, anal, and œdipal levels. In the process of working through, much of this ground has to be gone over again. The main task from the interpretive level at this time, however, has to do with establishing some mutually understandable language which can be a vehicle for providing insight concerning physical relatedness at a pre-verbal level of development. This can be a somewhat complicated task but in it the therapist is aided by the knowledge that the child has actually lived through an experience with him, one that carries its own physical logic and conviction.

Much now depends upon the child's home situation as to whether he can be discharged immediately or needs to be kept for a longer period at the school, seeing the therapist less and less frequently as he is weaned away. This is a matter of practical management, but I have frequently stressed the need to keep the child who has no home, or an extremely disturbed one, at the school for a considerable period in order that it may become perfectly clear to him that I am not rejecting him but that it is he who no longer has need of me.

With a new capacity to make meaningful relationships elsewhere it is only a matter of time before the child builds up a constellation of affects outside the clinical setting. One can then have confidence in discharging him.

13

Etiology

THE therapist who works with maladjusted and delinquent children cannot afford to ignore the classical techniques of psycho-analysis. Indeed the great majority of his time will be spent in working along traditional interpretive lines. This ground, however, has already been so well covered by others – Aichhorn, Bettelheim, Eissler, Anna Freud, Friedlander, Glover, Klein, Redl and Wineman, Schmideberg, Winnicott – that I have not attempted to detail it here.

What is remarkable about these children is that though they may be adolescent they react to the treatment situation in much the same way as the very small child in therapy: they cannot support the therapeutic process without at some time involving the therapist in close physical contact. We have, I think, to distinguish between two types of regression: the affective, and the psycho-physical. The adult patient in analysis may undergo a lengthy treatment without at any time moving from the couch or having need to touch or be touched by the analyst. Despite the physical distance that is preserved throughout, the patient may regress in mood, memory, and attitude to very early emotional states. This may be explained by the fact that intellectual and verbal mechanisms have become so highly developed and organized that words and ideas can carry the significance of primitive somatic experiences, or can at least be expressed with such facility as not to misrepresent the mood overmuch. This is broadly so with the neurotic patient and the manic-depressive, though it does not hold good with the psychotic who demands of the therapeutic agency actual physical care-taking procedures.

In this aspect the delinquent is closer to the psychotic patient in that mere affective regression, martialled by the treatment situation, the transference and traditional interpretive techniques, may be mutative over wide areas of the personality while at the same time leaving the central core of disturbance untouched. In order to resolve earlier intra-psychic distortions which are pre-genital and pre-verbal the treatment situation must allow for what I chose to call *psycho-physical regression*. What we find here is a recrudescence of a very primitive affective and somatic state in which contact with the mother's body was the only path by which the child could gain any real sense of 'me-ness' and 'other-ness', but in which the process of personal integration was not yet complete.

Regression here demands that there will be a brief period in which the child surrenders all self-caretaking procedures and permits the holding environment or the therapist to carry total responsibility as though the child were an incompletely differentiated part of a symbiotic whole. Only from this state, and by excited experimentation within it, can the child begin to establish a healthy awareness of himself as a total personality, and of other people as affectively meaningful objects not subject to his omnipotent control.

In the healthy mother-child relationship the mother is both *there* and is sufficiently stable to tolerate the strain resulting from impulsive behaviour and excited moods in the child; weaning is a gradual process and the establishment of 'distance' between mother and child is accomplished without traumatic urgency. Thus, though as time goes on the mother becomes less available, the child never feels that rejection is absolute nor that his instinctual impulses constitute a threat to her existence. Both hate and love are open to him in a person-to-person relationship and the child does not then have to establish excessive dependence upon things as part-substitutes for the mother, nor unduly limit his instinctual impulses in an attempt to preserve her.

In the delinquent child, on the other hand, it appears that the processes of weaning and disillusionment are carried through at so great a pace as to compel the child defensively to re-channel his impulses either: (a) into an over-evaluation of things to compensate for maternal loss; or (b) into destructive, hypermanic or aggressive behaviour as a technique which actively forces the environment to act against the child and so mitigate feelings of unreality.

Our experience of the parents of delinquent children leads us to conclude that in the main they are willing more than the average to use rejection as a technique of self-preservation, tend to wean their children earlier than most mothers,[1] and have little if any sensitivity to the anxiety and stress to which separation subjects the child. In this context rejection does not necessarily mean separation, for a mother may 'reject' her child by withdrawal of interest or affect as well as by actual neglect. For example, the mother who is depressed or excessively anxious, whether her anxiety or depression is directly related to the child or not, has withdrawn herself from him. Thus, at critical moments when the infant needs vital and lively physical contact with the external maternal object he finds himself in a partial vacuum. This must represent a severe trauma for the child, giving rise to anxiety, guilt, hate, or feelings of unreality. As a consequence of these processes the child's relationship with the outside world is thin, relatively colourless and hostile. Inwardly he organizes his feeling life around an injury and elaborates this with fantasy and a determination not to forgive.

In treatment, during the negative transference, we see all these processes in operation, but with hope. If, for example, we consider the case of Chris, whom I mentioned in the last chapter, it is clear that, once aggressive components were harnessed to the relationship, analytical interpretations and intellectual constructions neither added to nor subtracted from a dynamic situation which was carried forward by his capacity to sense my willingness to tolerate the total psycho-physical demands which he felt impelled to make upon me. Into this one experience were drawn all the primitive affective threads we have just enumerated: hate, guilt, murderous intent, guilt-reactive suicidal fantasies, an excited physical state, and loss of control. Again and again I have found the same concentration and condensation of violent and aggressive forces at the critical point of the negative transference.

The clinical task, therefore, in treating the delinquent child is to provide something more than insight and interpretation. It demands that the therapist be able to tolerate the excited aggression which the mother initially failed to meet. What limits success in such treatments is the precondition that the therapist shall have a sufficiently superior musculature as not to be threatened by the child's maniacal attack. For this reason I am convinced that the school for maladjusted children offers the child and the community one last chance of eradicating the anti-social tendency. If treat-

1. See Bennett, I., *Delinquent and Neurotic Children*. Tavistock, London, 1960, p.173-180.

ment is delayed too long the child will be the physical equal of the therapist. Muscular skill and co-ordination will have developed to the point where inner impulses can lead directly to dangerous action, thus constituting too great a threat to the therapist and making it more difficult if not impossible to examine the subjective meaning of the impulse itself.

This might explain why approved schools which cater for the older child have so high a percentage of recidivists and even their 'cured' pupils seem generally to have bartered any hope of personal health and integration for the one substantial gain of not becoming criminals.

It is not, of course, only in moods of aggression and fury that the therapist will find himself the object of the child's physical demands. The child will seek contact in all manner of moods – sad, pensive, gay, jocular, petulant – and will seek physical contact not only with the therapist but with any other transference-meaningful adult.

One psychotic boy who was in treatment with me for seven years – from the ages of eight to fifteen – went through a stage when he would spend most of each session curled up underneath my desk. Much of the time he would sit there sucking his fingers in silence. At other times he would draw 'pictures' which consisted in the main of concentric circles or spirals enclosing a vague object which in later sessions turned out to be an eye (a pun, I think, on the word 'I') and produce endless fantasies about birth and babies *in utero*. Later on he crammed as much of his body as he could under my chair and would talk to me or draw for me in that position. Gradually this developed into a charade in which he would wriggle his body out from under the chair between my legs. He would then lay his head on my lap and demand that I should feed him. Sometimes he would bring over slices of bread from the cottage and these I would crumble up and drop into his mouth. Most usually, however, I had to pour water which had had sugar added to it into his mouth. Occasionally at these times he would have identified himself so completely with an infant that he would pass urine in his trousers. He became enuretic at night also and for some long time conversed with me in 'baby talk'.

Following this phase very many sessions were spent during which he could talk to me only if he were sitting in a chair beside mine and leaning his body heavily against me with his head on my shoulder. When feeling particularly affectionate he would turn his head and lick my cheek. Eventually aggressive elements crept into his behaviour and he would bite or kick or scratch me.

I make brief mention of this boy, who made a full recovery, not because every boy carries regression to such lengths (being a psychotic he was not typical) but because his long and fascinating treatment demonstrates the many ways and moods in which the therapist may have to tolerate physical contact and is expected by the child to know why it is imperative that he should tolerate and understand what is going on.

These and similar observations have compelled me to conclude that in seeking the original predisposition towards delinquency we must trace a path back to some breakdown in the early mother-child relationship at a time when physical and psychic processes were as yet not stably differentiated.

14

Progress Report

IN an address given to a group of magistrates in 1946, Dr D. W. Winnicott spoke of the hostels for maladjusted children which had been set up during the war years. Of these hostels he said: 'Here, surely, is the place for the treatment of delinquency as an illness of the individual, and here, surely, is the place for research, and opportunity to gain experience. . . . In these hostels for the so-called maladjusted one is free to work with a therapeutic aim, and this makes a lot of difference. Failures will eventually come to the courts, but successes become citizens. . . .' And again: 'To return to the theme of children deprived of home life. Apart from being neglected (in which case they reach the juvenile courts as delinquents) they can be dealt with in two ways. They can be given personal psychotherapy, or they can be provided with a strong stable environment with personal care and love, and gradually increasing doses of freedom. As a matter of fact, without this latter the former (personal psychotherapy) is not likely to succeed.'[1]

Bredinghurst school, established two years later, was the first experimental attempt by any local authority to incorporate personal psychotherapy in a stable and sympathetic environment. Now, after eleven years of work, it is possible to make some kind of progress report on the methods tried. I do not propose to attempt a detailed statistical analysis which would, in any event, be meaningless since it has been impossible to set against the boys treated a control group of identically disturbed boys who have been given no treatment. But in 1953 Dr H. G. Williams, the L.C.C.'s consultant psychiatrist, undertook a statistical comparison between boys actually at Bredinghurst who had received analytical treatment, and those who had not. He based his investigation on six points:

1. *The Child and the Outside World.* Tavistock, London, 1957, p.185f.

151

(1) the child's improved relationship to parents and authorities;
(2) improved capacity to learn;
(3) an expansion in the child's interest;
(4) improved social relationships;
(5) less inhibited but better controlled aggression;
(6) loss or diminution of symptoms present on admission.

Marks were awarded for the following four degrees of change:

> No change, scoring 0
> Slight improvement, scoring 1
> Fair improvement, scoring 2
> Marked or complete improvement, scoring.... 3

The result of this comparison are as follows:

> Treated children .... Mean 17.0
> Untreated children .... Mean 11.9

The difference is statistically significant.

Dr Williams commented on his investigation: 'The results so far achieved by this investigation are interesting. . . . It will also be appreciated that there is no sharp line of demarcation between the treated and untreated groups. These are not separated into watertight compartments; the school staff often consult the psychiatric staff on children who are not under treatment, and these are given occasional interviews. On the whole the tendency is for the more difficult of the internally disturbed children to be selected for psychiatric treatment. The existence of the psychiatric unit has affected the whole school. . . . The school staff have tended to develop an enquiring and non-critical attitude to the boy's problems rather than concentrating on securing standards of conduct. . . .'

Dr Williams further stated that he was: 'firmly of the opinion that the results observed so far in the school indicate that the subsequent behaviour of those boys who have received psychiatric treatment because of their marked degree of maladjustment is now as good as, and in some ways better than, those who have not been treated. Furthermore those [adults] who have been connected with the experiment are convinced of the value of the work that has been done, and feel that the time has come for psychiatric treatment to be regarded as an important and regular feature of the Council's provision for selected maladjusted children in boarding special schools.'

Statistics and observations of this kind, useful as they are, fail to reflect many aspects of the work. Nor do they indicate certain vital factors which I intend to discuss in this context. First, over the years the age on admittance of the boys at Bredinghurst has steadily risen. At one time we were admitting children of six and seven. In recent years, however, the age on admittance has been eleven or twelve. A great deal happens to a child during the five or six years that elapse from the time he might have been sent to us till the time he actually arrives at the school. Each attempt the child makes in those years to find an understanding environment will have met with failure and this inevitably thrusts him back again into despair, makes him suspicious of the adult world's willingness or capacity to help him, reinforces his psychic defence mechanisms. In addition he will possibly have been to court once or twice, so that should he become delinquent while at Bredinghurst he already has a court history which is inclined to bias the magistrates against further tolerance.

More important from our point of view, the actual physical problem of handling a thirteen-year-old boy is a very different thing from dealing with a seven year old. Very many deprived children, as they begin to recover from depression, become aggressive, have maniacal attacks of uncontrollable excitement, or may give themselves over to a short fury of destructiveness. It must be observed that a severe disadvantage of the older adolescent age-group is that they are already involved in a new biological developmental crisis which complicates the clinical picture further and lends a new urgency to their defensive and flight techniques.

There is the further complication that to admit older children puts a very definite time-limit on the possible duration of treatment. It is not permitted for us to keep a boy in the school beyond his sixteenth birthday. Since we have found that the average length of treatment necessary is somewhere between three and four years we know from the start with the older boys that we have not time to undertake more than comparatively superficial therapy. In many cases this has been encouragingly successful, but it does mean that we are being pressed to the limit.

The second major factor in this context is that as time has gone on Bredinghurst has established a reputation as a treatment centre. In consequence of this courts, hospital clinics, child guidance units, and social workers have been inclined to recommend the more disturbed children to us. We have also had to admit from other L.C.C. schools boys who have deteriorated under ordinary management. Had they been sent to us in the first place treatment might have been a comparatively simple matter. By the time we eventually get them the prognosis may be very poor.

It has thus come about that over the last decade Bredinghurst has gradually come to admit not only older children, but also the more seriously disturbed type of child. These two factors have inevitably had an adverse effect upon the percentage of boys discharged as cured. Besides these major disadvantages it has to be borne in mind that at the outset none of the staff had had any experience of working in exactly this kind of close liaison with other disciplines, there were no special training facilities for teachers or house-staff, and rather too high a proportion of resident staff stayed for comparatively short periods in the school.

Several years of working need to elapse before a school psychiatric team gains sufficient confidence to know not only the types of child it is able to treat but also those who are unlikely to benefit. Our own uncertainty resulted, in the early days, in a number of boys being admitted who would have been better placed in hospitals or other schools, e.g., schizophrenic and educationally subnormal children.

I must emphasize once more that the effects of psychotherapy are not confined to boys receiving regular treatment. Any boy in the school is at liberty to ask for an occasional hour with the therapist. He is also free to discuss his home and personal problems with the psychiatric social worker, and he is seen from time to time by the consulting psychiatrist. Over and above these opportunities is the fact that the presence of the psychiatric team within the school has a marked effect upon the total atmosphere, upon the attitudes of each member of the staff and, indirectly therefore, on every boy whether he is himself in treatment or not.

Leaving out of account boys who were removed from our care within a month by their parents, we have admitted and discharged in these eleven years 216 boys. By all ascertainable standards 181 boys (84 per cent.) have made a reasonably normal readjustment to life outside the school, at home or in work; 27 have been admitted to approved schools or Borstals either direct from Bredinghurst or as a result of some delinquent action after discharge from the school, the other 8, while not in approved schools, hospitals or Borstals, are felt to be managing their lives with some difficulty and may at a future date need further institutional care. It should be noted that the rate of committal to approved schools declined markedly as Bredinghurst became more firmly established and as the team gained in experience. The majority of these commitals took place during the first four years. Of the 78 boys who have received sustained psychotherapy 4 have been admitted to approved schools. One of these was committed by a magistrate's court when he had been resident with us for only one year and despite our conviction that he was showing marked improvement.

It is difficult to determine what exactly are the criteria of a 'cure', a suspect word in itself. In compiling these figures we have considered the child's adaptation to life and new situations in as broad a context as possible and submit that we have established beyond reasonable doubt that maladjustment can be treated and that the deprived and delinquent child need not be regarded as a permanent incubus on society.

We do not 'treat' delinquency any more than we 'treat' enuresis. Our aim is something more than that. We aim to find a path back for the deprived child to normal health, to a positive state of mind in which he can accept responsibility for himself, tolerate inner tensions from conflicts, act responsibly towards the community, trust in the goodwill of others, and establish sound and meaningful relationships with his peers and with adults. We do not seek merely to prevent these children from becoming a burden on the community, but rather to liberate those hopeful and positive elements in their psychological equipment which will enable them to become healthy citizens.

If the boys who have passed through this school, despite the emotional turmoil of their early years, are able to fit themselves for a job, to enjoy ordinary human pleasures, to live comparatively free from crippling anxieties and depressions, to marry happily and become affectionate and responsible parents, then the work we have done will have been well done. It will, however, be necessary in the future to institute research and follow-up systems to gauge more accurately the results of our work and to compare these with the results obtained by non-therapeutic schools. The ultimate measure of the success or failure of a school of this type will be seen only when the boys we have treated have become adults and themselves fathered a new generation, for unresolved delinquent tendencies in the parent are so often 'acted out' in the child.

It would be wrong to suggest that we are satisfied with what success has been achieved. By no means all our failures have been in direct relationship with the children. We have not been successful in establishing a corps of well-trained staff willing to devote the majority of their working or professional life to this one school. It is essential, if it is to function at its best, that there should be few staff changes. Therapy depends for its efficacy to a very large extent upon the child's capacity to feel that the adults in the school are as settled a feature of the environment as a mother and father are in a normal home. Whenever one or other adult leaves the school the effect of this shift in the environment is immediately reflected in the behaviour of one or more of the boys.

In our view it is essential to establish conditions which make it possible for the staff to feel settled, to view this as their career, a more or less permanent appointment – and here we have failed. Nor has the school been wholly successful in creating an atmosphere in which sufficient 'mothering' can be offered to those boys most in need of it. The disturbed child needs at certain moments of personal crisis to feel that he can draw upon the undiluted attention of one adult or another. He may only need to be comforted when he wakes in the night, or he may be in need of special contact with an understanding adult for many hours at a time. So long as the school is organized in rather large groups of fifteen or more in each cottage, it is virtually impossible for the various staff members to meet this need adequately. It seems to us important that groups should be broken down into family-sized units which not only create a permanent feeling of intimacy between the child and the house-parents but also permit him to feel that he is not making an unreasonable demand at times of special stress.

In summary, Bredinghurst has been:
  conspicuously successful in supplying the physical needs of the boys in our care;
  successful in protecting the community from the delinquent and disturbing behaviour of the children;
  successful to a gratifying extent in curing the emotional disorders from which these children suffer;
  tolerably successful in bringing about a genuine and positive reorientation in the skills and attitudes of the teaching and non-professional staff;
  and unsuccessful in persuading all members of the educational administration of the singular complexity of creating and sustaining a therapeutic environment.

15

Perspective

MEN have always acted in manners irreconcilable with their convictions concerning goodness and justice. Not until 1885, however, when Freud developed the concept of the dynamic unconscious, was it possible to begin to explore the inner logic behind the predicament and paradox outlined by St Paul: 'For the good that I would I do not; but the evil which I would not, that I do.'[1] This is apposite when reflecting on the evolution of the psychiatric approach to behavioural disorders. During its first decades psychoanalysis was occupied in charting the territory of hysteria and transference neuroses, and there was very little incentive to apply therapeutic techniques to delinquents or to disturbed and anti-social children. While psycho-analysts were thus engaged in establishing the dynamics of psychotherapy, delinquency and maladjustment continued to be treated in terms of their sociological and moral aspects. Hence remedial measures varied from indulgence and pity to corrective discipline.

Starting with his researches into melancholia (1917) and the ego's response to loss-experiences, Freud arrived at his structural definition of the personality into id, superego, and ego (1923). This in turn led to his revision of the theory of anxiety in 1926. Here the affect of anxiety, instead of being merely a translation of dammed-up libido into anxiety, was envisaged as a signal reaction on the part of the ego to all situations entailing insecurity, loss of the loved object, or punitive threats. This work opened up the researches into character disorders (Alexander, Reich).

In the past it had been assumed that delinquency was the result of a weak or inadequate conscience, and strenuous efforts were made by means of threats, re-education, and persuasion to reform the wrong-doer. With increasing insight into super-ego formation

1. Romans, vii, 19.

and unconscious primitive guilt reactions (Freud, Alexander[2], Klein[3], Glover[4]) it became possible to see delinquent acts, aggressive anti-social traits, and generalized behavioural disorders as an essential element in the maladjusted child's attempts to ward off unbearable inner tension and thus keep in touch with reality. Furthermore, understanding of primitive aggressive impulses and their role in the sadistic super-ego formation enabled one to appraise more correctly the function of behavioural disorders as a technique for warding off panic, depression, emotional stupor, and diffuse guilt-feelings.

It now became increasingly clear that only an understanding examination of these underlying conflicts could possibly yield genuine insight into the psychic constitution of the disturbed child. This approach became imperative because in maladjustment the flight from reality seldom takes the psychotic form of complete withdrawal into a world of hallucination, nor the neurotic form of isolation and repression through overt symptom formation.[5] Rather does the maladjusted child preserve a pose of normality and apparently vivid contact with reality. But this contact with reality is illusive for it is based upon magical and omnipotent conceptions through which he seeks to adapt reality to his fantasies rather than his fantasies to reality[6] The secondary gains to the child through this inner psychic manœuvre play a very negative role in the willingness of these children to be helped – a fact which has often been mistaken for an evil bias in their nature rather than a further symptom of distress.

Another anomaly of the emotionally disturbed child's seemingly cogent sense of reality, his wide areas of rational behaviour, his clear understanding of what is good and what is bad, what is right and what is wrong, is that if on one hand it produces hope in those responsible for him, on the other hand it also reduces the individuals in the environment to quick despair on account of the unpredictable eruptions of unconscious needs and conflicts on which, and against which, his sense of reality has little hold.

2. Alexander, F., and Staub, H., *The Criminal, the Judge and the Public*. Allen & Unwin, London, 1931 and Alexander, F., and Healy, W., *The Roots of Crime*. Knopf, New York, 1935.
3. *The Psycho-analysis of Children*. Hogarth, London, 1932.
4. *The Roots of Crime*. Imago, London, 1960.
5. See Eissler's paper in *Searchlights on Delinquency*. Imago, London, 1949, p.3f.
6. Klein, M., *Contributions to Psycho-analysis*. Hogarth, London, 1945, p.195.

Thus the delinquent's profound belief in magic and omnipotence, which are his only means of coping with inner desolation and acute anxieties, drive him to actions which have as their aim the complete mastery of the external world. This psychic pattern has nothing in common with normal straining after success and personal achievement, though it may often appear to be the same thing. The delinquent needs must, therefore, view other people not as persons in themselves, but only as objects to be used to further his own ends. These ends are determined by the defiance elements and the compulsion on the one hand aggressively to degrade the loved object to the level of a mere receptacle for instinctual drives, yet on the other they carry the regressive need to return to a primitive stage of object-love where the mother is essentially the satisfier of 'greedy stomach-love'.[7] The integration of these two processes within the setting provided by the school creates the greatest challenge and task for those dealing with the maladjusted child. This conflictual constellation in the child is further illustrated by his acute ambivalence to male figures which derives from the bisexual elements in his libidinal impulses. He attempts to resolve his conflict on a phallic-narcissistic basis by gang-formation and thus is deprived of the positive gains from a more passive identification with father-figures, and also of that enrichment of the ego which is dependent upon the neutralization and sublimation of more passive feminine strivings. This further preconditions the maladjusted child towards identifications with hostile aggressive figures to whom he has a great deal of access in the modern cinema and the comic strip, as well as in his own bizarre family setting. This compulsion towards projective identifications with the aggressor (Anna Freud, 1936) further intensifies the anti-social behavioural traits in these children.

If we now shift our attention to the genetic causes of these disturbances we find that at the heart of the problem lie actual traumatic experiences in the family, which the child has progressively and retrospectively interpreted to himself in terms of an acute sense of injustice. It is important to be able to differentiate this from the neurotic patient's fantasies that he was, for instance, loved less than another sibling. *The maladjusted child has proper cause to believe that he has been the victim of a real deprivation or injustice.*

7. Freud, A., *The Psycho-analytical Study of the Child*. Imago, London: vol. 8, p.17.

This injustice may have taken one of many forms. It may be an actual rejection by the mother, or rejection through unconscious conflicts in the parents. It may be rejection or deprivation through the parents' inability to meet a particularly oversensitive child's particular needs; hence we have the phenomenon that only one of many children in a family may become maladjusted. In other instances an emotional factor – e.g. loss of a parent, physical illness in one of the parents, economic crises, illness in the child himself or in another sibling – can so disturb the family setting as to create exaggerated anxiety and insecurity in the child, to which he reacts with excessive demands for help which the environment cannot meet and to which it may react with either overt or unconscious rejection.[8]

In our experience we have found it of the utmost importance both diagnostically and therapeutically to recognize that maladjustment is not merely the result of intra-psychic splits between the id, ego, and the super-ego or archaic super-ego functioning. Our experience suggests that the root cause of maladjustment and antisocial behaviour lies in a three-way reaction of the child's primitive ego to specific traumatic experiences *vis-à-vis* his environment. These reactions in time becomes organized as inner dissociated states:

(1) The child grows normally to a certain point in ego-development till, at a crucial phase, there is an actual environmental failure, an act of injustice, or a genuine deprivation which has a traumatic effect on the child (Winnicott, 1945, 1949). This traumatic effect then leads regressively to a confusion of ego- and id-values in which on the one hand the child precociously tries to compensate to his environment on which he is dependent, and on the other internalizes his personal experience of being failed and nurses himself inwardly, and with maturation exploits his ego-capacity to fight and fend off any intrusion into this self-care-taking structure. This inner stress leads to a precocious, archaic, and sadistic super-ego formation which then compels acts of restitution or creates anxieties of retribution which lie

8. See Freud's discussion of trauma in *Moses and Monotheism*. Knopf, New York, 1939. M. M. Stern's discussion of infantile traumata in the *International Journal of Psycho-analysis*: vol. 38, p.146ff. See also Bowlby John, *Maternal Care and Mental Health*. World Health Organization, Geneva, 1951.

behind so many of the bizarre and defiant acts of the maladjusted child.

(2) The restitutive element is readily visible to anyone who has observed such children in their pathetic attempts to help their parents, and their acute humiliation (unconscious) and lack of self-esteem at failing to do so.

(3) The self-protective and compensatory elements one detects in the inability of these children to trust their environment to care for and help them.

The dissociations in the ego and the resultant weakness lead to exaggerated and even bizarre eruptions of id-tensions or equally severe sadistic super-ego conflicts, the ego then having to resort to further defences of a primitive type to cope with the new burden of anxiety. Only too often this resultant behaviour is mistaken as an end in itself. These primitive defence mechanisms lead to typical behavioural disorders, either over-sexualized or over-aggressive, their gradual development resulting in a secondary logic of their own, which the society sees as the identity of the child.

Until such time as the need for these defences is modified or alleviated in a therapeutic environment and by psychotherapy the child's survival and total security depend upon their preservation.[9] Clinically the problem is to enable the child to come to the point where he can live without having to rely on these defence mechanisms which have, so far, been his sole security.

One can schematically differentiate the ordinary environment's reactions, in order to help or control the maladjusted child, into two categories which are in no small measure guided by the splits in the child's inner world and ego:

(a) The environment may take on a disciplinary role. If the child is receptive to it (which is not very often) then he may achieve a temporary relief in his condition through introjection of new benign super-ego figures which help him allay inner archaic sources of guilt and anxiety. Thus a temporary balance on sadistic-masochistic terms might easily emerge.

9. Stern, M. M., *International Journal of Psycho-analysis*: vol. 38, p.147. 'We may conceive of the human mental apparatus as a grandiose extension of the processes that safeguard homeostatic equilibrium and the survival of the individual.'

(b) The environment may be benignly permissive. If too permissive, however, the child can exploit it as a source of new and vicarious id-satisfactions which can lead to a pleasurable eroticization of anxiety as a defence against inner conflicts. This is often the cause of the proclivity of these children to perversions through seduction.

Either of these measures can link up with the child's inner self-compensatory processes and attempts at self-cure, but they do not help him in the resolution of those conflicts and needs which are at the root of his problems and may do no more than confuse the clinical picture.

This also explains why it is that children who are submitted to, and submit themselves to, a rigidly moralistic régime almost invariably prove a disappointment to themselves or to their caretaking environment. Even if they should succeed in maintaining a façade of good citizenship they continue to feel futile and paralysed in their subjective experience. This persistence of inner unresolved needs and conflicts then become visible only through a feeling of deadness or boredom or lack of personal initiative.

Correspondingly, if the solution has been on id-gratification lines, one finds these children compulsively seeking this type of relief through discharge without the instinctual experiences achieving any personal value or significance for them. In this constellation aggressive, over-sexualized or anti-social behaviour is unavoidable and may persist indefinitely until at some point it compels society to act in a self-protective way against the individual. The regression here is to primitive id-levels where pregenital patterns predominate. The maladjusted child's attempt to cope with this intrusion of id-content through displacement on to ego-functions has been valuably discussed by Anna Freud.[10]

It is the central contention throughout this volume that any attempt which aims at helping the maladjusted child resolve his conflicts or change his reactive behaviour patterns, and thus find the freedom to discover his personal identity and integration, must not fall into either of the two pitfalls I have outlined above – over-discipline or over-permissiveness. Recovery to full emotional health can be achieved only by the provision of a new environment (the school) which can make good the original deprivation, and by

10. *Searchlights on Delinquency*. Imago, London, 1949.

psychotherapy within this setting bring about a correction of the ego-distortion and primitive defence mechanisms. A resolution of these ego-splits only becomes possible within an environment which is able to compensate the child for his original loss by the provision of an integrated and whole setting.

It is my contention that where a school is able to provide the child with a positive environment *and* psychotherapy it is possible to avoid the split in the patient's ego being reflected in the adult handling of the situation.

In maladjustment and delinquency there are both autoplastic and alloplastic elements, with the latter in ascendency. In the past there have been two alternative methods of attempting treatment – environmental care which recognizes the alloplastic elements and seeks to deal with the problem through interplay between the child and his setting, and psycho-analytical techniques which aim at trying 'to change the proportion of the two sets of elements in favour of the autoplastic', thus putting treatment into the familiar context of analysis of neuroses.[11]

In our experience both these techniques permit the environment to enter into a collusion – consciously in the case of analysis, unconsciously in the case of the educationists – with the split in the child's personality. The advantage of the therapeutic school which incorporates psychotherapy as a dynamic function of the school itself is that it neither exploits nor denies the ego-split in the patient. The inner dissociations thus become a practical task which the total setting has to resolve.

In a succinct statement, Willi Hoffer writes: 'Perhaps we should regard the interplay between self and object as the central paradox of emotional development: *that the child needs his mother's love in order to be able to love himself*, in order to be able to do without her love; then he should be able to love another person as he was loved by his mother'[12] (my italics). Psychotherapy becomes effective only if there is a setting which takes over the role of making love real to these children. The one fact which has been accepted by all disciplines about the maladjusted child is his actual deficiency of experiences of being loved and cared for in infancy and early childhood. Thus it seems logical that the provision of love and the pro-

11. Eissler, K. R., ibid. p.17.
12. Williams and Wilkins, *Psycho-analysis*. Baltimore, 1955, p.91.

vision of psychotherapy should be integrated as inseparable elements of any attempt to resolve the problem.

It is a remarkable fact that the two disciplines or philosophies which have taken a live interest in the plight of the deprived child, the delinquent, and the social outcast – Christianity and psychoanalysis – each in its own way has emphasized the healing effect of love. While the religio-social worker offers love and confidently expects the child to accept it, be grateful, repent and reform, the analyst, by contrast, recognizes that these children are, at the outset at least, quite incapable of accepting love on any terms and that the first task is to break down the defences which the child has erected against the invasion of his personality by that of others and by inner needs. The analyst also allows for the fact that vast quantities of repressed hate will and must emerge and be resolved into personal behaviour before any capacity to give and receive love can become a dynamic reality to the child. Oddly enough at present it is analysis, which is not a sentimental technique and which recognizes the dynamic of aggression and hatred as well as of love, that is engaged in trying to persuade a society based on the Christian ethic to act in a more loving manner towards the anti-social child.

The danger of the religio-social point of view is that love unreturned quickly becomes metamorphosed into unconscious hatred. To love and expect love in return, but to be greeted only with resentment and increased delinquency, is to lose faith in one's self, in one's convictions, and in the object of one's concern. This is the tragic dilemma so often and so quickly arrived at by many well-intentioned persons who find themselves drawn into work with the disturbed child. In the event they become more and more repressive in their methods, more cynical about their failures, and more convinced that delinquency is an inborn criminal tendency which can be rendered impotent only by re-education in an oppressive environment.

The therapist, by contrast, recognizing from the start that the problem is not how to love but how to make love real, does not set out from a point of sanguine confidence. Unlike a teacher, who may wish to inculcate ideals and standards of acceptable behaviour in the child, the therapist aims to learn *from the child* the reasons lying at the back of his personal predicament. The psychotherapist undertakes a task; the religio-social worker begins with a determined hope. The psychotherapist sets out to discover the full range of the unconscious expectancy in the child, while the religio-social worker and the pure educationist tend to impose an expectancy on the child.

The worker who begins with the conviction that love is enough, by excluding other approaches, limits his own freedom and creativity. The therapist offers strength, critical examination, a ruthless dialogue of personal encounter, even hatred in its context, and love through the idiom of sympathy and understanding which alone makes it meaningful and acceptable.

The therapist, however, must recognize and allow for the fact that what he does can be done at its best only in a school setting which cares for the child every day and all day. Only so long as this continued care is there for the child to nurture himself on, and depend upon, and for the therapist to relate to the patient's inner situation, can the work of the therapist, in short clinical sessions, have full significance and lasting value. That successful treatment depends to a remarkable degree upon the therapist's ability to capitalize the provision and care offered to the child by the school cannot be overemphasized.

The therapist may achieve a great deal in the brief hours at his disposal, but the significance of these critical hours cannot be divorced from the therapeutic benefit which accrues from the fact that, for the other twenty-three hours in the day, the child can depend upon an encompassing and positive environment which is provided by the teaching and house-staff.

The guiding principles of the work reported in this book may be briefly expressed in the following propositions:

I. Maladjustment and delinquency involve two basic elements:
   (a) genetically, an actual deprivation in childhood;
   (b) dynamically and currently, an acute distortion in ego-development and personality integration.

II. Any adequate treatment that aims at meeting and correcting the disorders of maladjustment and delinquency must be designed to meet the above factors by:
   (a) making good the initial experiential deficiency, which is possible only in a stable setting – it is here that educationists

and psychotherapists not only can but must work in close association; and

(b) the provision of adequate psychotherapy which alone can help the child to gain insight into and resolve his conflicts, unconscious anxieties, and reactive character traits.

16

Recommendations

OVER the decade under review I believe we have established that it is possible to treat successfully the maladjusted and delinquent child in a structured setting. We have further satisfied ourselves that it is possible for the educationist and the psychotherapist to work in close association, and that the contribution of the psychiatric team is not confined to the treatment of the individual child but assists in the creation of a special environment in which cure is more certain and in which the whole school becomes a therapeutic unit. In this we support the contention of Dr John Bowlby[1] who said of the treatment of maladjusted children – 'It has three aspects: (a) the utilization of the total social group for therapeutic ends; (b) the development of a therapeutic relationship with a staff member; (c) the provision of individual psychotherapy or counselling.'

The need of the child to establish dependence upon one or more of the staff and to use this relationship both regressively and positively has been emphasized in this report, and we are convinced that unless the school can make provision for this need little advantage will accrue to the child. On the other hand we are equally convinced that affectionate care on the part of the environment and regressive phenomena on the part of the child cannot of themselves restore health in the majority of cases. It is of great advantage to the adult and an absolute necessity for the child to gain insight into the internal psychic processes, an insight which can be gained only through analytical techniques.

It has been encouraging for the psychiatric team to discover with what avidity the majority of teaching and house-staff have sought an increased understanding of their dynamic role. The amalgama-

1. *Maternal Care and Mental Health.* World Health Organization, Geneva, 1951, p.143.

tion of educational, child-care, and therapeutic techniques has enabled the school as a whole to articulate more clearly than it could otherwise have done its central purpose, to gain a greater tolerance of anxiety, and thus permit the child to regress to primitive states of dependence, resolve infantile conflicts, and then bring forward into the present the fundamental satisfactions he has gained.

We have further been able to show that only through the medium of the therapeutic setting and of analytical interpretation does a really stable ego-organization emerge in the child which can tolerate id-tensions, inner conflicts, and the creative use of personal and social values. These conclusions having been reached, there are a number of practical recommendations that must be stated.

(1) There are those who feel that, since it is axiomatic that the psychiatrist and the therapist have a greater knowledge of maladjustment than has the teaching staff, schools of this kind should be under psychiatric direction. From the point of view of the psychiatric team such a structure would have obvious advantages. They would be able to assist in selecting new teaching and house-staff and no administrative decision would be made without regard to the main therapeutic aim. The danger of such a course would be the tendency to transform these schools into hospitals, thereby emphasizing the child's illness and isolation from ordinary life and his 'difference' from other children.

Critics have said that education authorities and school committees elected from among ordinary citizens without special knowledge are not the persons best suited to run schools for maladjustment. Not all county councillors and administrators are capable of the high level of tolerance, understanding and anxiety which this work demands, and they are very sensitive to shifts in the popular attitude towards psychiatry and the handling of the delinquent. In consequence, some of the best and more sustained work in this field has so far been achieved by independent schools which are largely immune to such influences and have been built around the personality of one talented individual.

It would seem to me, however, that any action on the part of the psychiatrists which might transform the school into a 'residential clinic' is to be deplored. These establishments should, first and foremost, be schools. On the other hand psychiatrists and therapists cannot be expected to tolerate a situation, should it arise, in which their views and opinions may be ignored and their wishes disregarded by educationists whose knowledge of the medical problems involved is minimal and whose personal bias against psychiatry could render the work of the psychiatric team virtually valueless.

In practice it is seldom that conflict arises between teaching and psychiatric staff where a headmaster and the administration share a determination to further the therapeutic aim of the school. Our experience indicates that the best work is done when the school is running efficiently as a school, with a good and conscientious teaching staff who are sufficiently well-versed in child-care theory and technique to wish to co-operate with the psychiatric team. As time goes on and an increasing proportion of the teaching staff choose to take special courses in the treatment of maladjusted children, it should be possible to bring about a high level of imaginative co-operation between the two disciplines.

(2) For reasons set out on pages 24-26 it is advisable that these schools should be set up in the city, within easy reach of the homes of the children.

(3) To be therapeutically effective the school must reproduce as nearly as possible the good home situation, for only under such conditions can the child establish meaningful relationships with adults which will parallel or reduplicate a healthy parent-child relationship. There is an unhealthy tendency still for some of these establishments to retain the characteristics of an institution. Anything like regimentation, martial discipline, uniformity in dress, obsessional standards in cleanliness, insistence on implicit obedience will militate against a positive attachment between child and adult.

Incredible as it must seem, there are still schools for maladjusted children in which the house-staff have to fill in a form each morning, putting a tick against each boy's name as he washes his face does his hair, folds his blankets, cleans his shoes, etc. Children in these schools are compelled, when undressing at night, to take off their clothes in a particular order and lay them out beside their beds in a certain order from which they must not deviate. Obsessional attitudes and regulations of this kind expose the pathetic poverty of the technical training of some of the workers in this field. Nothing could be further removed from the normal home environment; nothing could be better designed to convince the child of the arid, impersonal, and hostile nature of the administration.

(4) In common with so many other workers with disturbed children I am inclined to think that the cottage system in which a small number of children live together in a house, under the care of permanently assigned house-staff, is the arrangement best suited to residential schools. Even though at Bredinghurst each of these units consisted of fifteen boys, we found it was possible for them to establish a close dependence upon the house-parents and for the staff to develop a keen affection towards the children. The establishment and uninterrupted maintenance of these relationships is an essential element in the therapeutic school. Ideally each cottage should be in the charge of a married couple in order that the normal family structure may be reproduced. Since household chores are undertaken by the domestic staff it is possible for the house-mother to do all the cooking. As in an ordinary home, the children wake to the sound and smell of bacon being fried downstairs and dine throughout the day in small family groups.

Any way in which the cottage-parent can assume the parental role will be of lasting value to the child. It is essential, therefore, that the staff bedrooms should be in the cottages. If a child wakes in the night there must be someone to answer his call. Much depends upon there being an adequate supply of stable staff to undertake these duties. The parental role cannot be sustained if the cottage-group is too large (and fifteen should be regarded as the absolute maximum), or where the staff are placed on a rota system which inevitably dilutes the close relationship that should exist. The child-care staff who have worked at Bredinghurst have been unanimous in the opinion that the rota system not only undermines the child-adult relationship but destroys the personal satisfaction which the staff themselves hope to gain from their work.

(5) The total school population should be kept at a low figure. The normal complement at Bredinghurst is forty-five boys. If the school is dealing with severely disturbed children perhaps even this figure is rather too high. So vitally important is the personal nature of the work and the need for the headmaster to keep in close touch with each child and parent that I am inclined to think that a total of thirty-five boys in residence ought not to be exceeded.

Local authorities are clearly aiming not so much to find the maximum number of places in the minimum space of time as to ensure that a truly therapeutic unit be established and then duplicated elsewhere. It may be argued that to adopt such a course is to increase the per capita cost of residential treatment. Against this must be set the fact that better results are obtained from the smaller units and, consequently, fewer boys will find their way to approved schools, Borstals, and prisons.

(**6**) The size of classes in the school must also be kept small. Many maladjusted children have a high intelligence and are often more sensitive than the average child. Not to provide them with a sound educational programme to which they can respond as they improve in emotional health is merely to increase their sense of frustration and anxiety – anxiety and frustration which are likely to result in aggressive and anti-social behaviour.

The disturbed child needs much individual attention in class. In a large class he feels nervous and out-of-touch with adults. In order to gain the attention and reassuring contact he requires, a small tutorial group is necessary. A class of more than eight disturbed children is virtually unmanageable unless the teacher has recourse to near-Victorian methods of discipline and learning by rote. The maladjusted child is markedly more restless than is the normal child, emotional tension being expressed in physical volatility. He is also less able to concentrate on academic work over long periods.

(**7**) Careful selection of cases is essential if the school is to make the best use of the services it has to offer. From time to time certain boys have been admitted to Bredinghurst who have proved to be psychotic or whose delinquency has been a neurotic symptom rather than a sign of maladjustment. A school is not equipped to deal with psychotic patients, and the neurotic child is best treated by analytical methods while continuing to live in his own home. Skilled diagnosis should ensure that residential treatment is reserved for maladjusted children only.

(**8**) The local authority should, I believe, institute regulations whereby it is possible for them to claim from the parents of all children a reasonable proportion of the cost of keeping the child in the school. Not only would this serve to reduce the heavy expenditure on the public purse which such schools involve, but it would also ensure that in no way can it be thought that the local authority aims to oust the parents or drive a wedge between the child and his home.

(9) Much has yet to be done to attract into these schools adult personnel who are possessed of adequate training and personal qualities which fit them for work with maladjusted children. The teacher who has no qualification other than the teacher's training certificate is at a very real disadvantage when working in an environment which makes exacting demands on his time, personality and skill, which calls for continual study, for wide and intelligent reading, and a 'research attitude' to the job. An intuitive feeling for the child, while an advantage, is no substitute for knowledge or training.

Schools for maladjusted children ought to be able to attract the very best type of teacher. Given sufficient knowledge of what the work has to offer the individual both intellectually and emotionally, I am convinced that talented and able men and women can be increasingly drawn into this field, for it offers enormous scope for the alert and imaginative individual. At the moment not nearly enough teachers of the requisite high calibre are coming forward, a situation which is causing grave concern to the administration.

Discussing the organization of treatment centres for emotionally disturbed children Bovet writes:

> A serious stumbling block is the anxiety of many re-educators when first collaborating with a psychiatrist, an anxiety which easily changes into reactive aggression. Surprised by the complex processes revealed by the psychiatrist, disconcerted by knowledge of the delinquent's paradoxical reactions, the re-educator, overwhelmed by feelings of impotence and ignorance, will either give up, or take refuge more than ever in classical and superficial methods of schooling whose simplicity reassures him.[2] Given opportunities for specialised training, the risk of this type of reaction among teachers will be considerably reduced.

Psycho-analytical theories are now so well established and so broadly accepted that it should not be impossible to recruit men and women who are in sympathy with the analytical point of view and eager to relate psychiatric insight to their own tasks. It does not seem to me practicable, or even advisable, that all workers in these

2. *Juvenile Delinquency*. World Health Organization, Geneva, 1951.

schools should have themselves been analysed. There is great need and scope for the simple, human, motherly or fatherly type of person whose affectionate identification with the child is completely unself-conscious.

(10) The position of the psychiatric staff in these schools is not always a happy one. Intolerance or hostility may show itself in ways which gravely limit the therapist and run counter to the development of a therapeutic milieu. Perhaps the next step that needs to be taken is to assure psychiatric workers that they are truly welcomed in these schools by the authorities and to permit them some say in selection of staff and administrative decisions. At Bredinghurst in the past all appointments have been made without consultation with psychiatric staff. In the main these appointments have proved wise, but occasionally a man or woman has been employed who was clearly unfitted for the work and prior consultation with the psychiatrist might have avoided the resultant complications.

When selecting either teaching or house-staff certain very real character and behavioural disorders have to be guarded against. Discussing this problem, Bovet[3] writes: 'Most important of all, only the emotionally stable should be employed. Particular care should be taken to eliminate any psychopaths and psychoneurotics, who are only too often attracted to the re-education of these anti-social youths by a sort of positive tropism which must be uncovered. The following personalities should likewise be eliminated: homosexuals, either overt or with strong latent tendencies, the dissatisfied, the over-possessive, the more or less openly sadistic and masochistic; in short, all whose activity in a reform institution, on careful psychological examination . . . seems to serve a biological function necessary to satisfy their own neuroses, rather than the desire to be of service to a social ideal.' It may not be possible for the headmaster, or in the case of the selection of a headmaster the management committee of a school, to give the requisite 'careful psychological examination' since they lack the necessary skill to detect quite glaring character faults in an applicant, faults which might be more readily detected by a psychiatrist.

(11) The value of developing and preserving the adult working unit as a team cannot be overstressed and I would suggest that whenever new staff have to be appointed the wishes of the rest of the staff should be taken into consideration. It has come to my

3. ibid. p.68.

notice that in one approved school, for example, when a new teacher has to be appointed, the various applicants' names and qualifications are submitted to the whole staff for their criticisms and comments, and it is the staff themselves who draw up the short-list of applicants from which the final selection is made. This, it would seem, is a very positive step, aimed at ensuring that the team as a whole feel that any alteration in the composition of the school takes place only after consultation with those who work in the setting. Such a course, if generally adopted, might do much to avoid the unfortunate situation which can so easily develop where the administration or the headmaster appoints members to the staff who lack the capacity to work harmoniously with the established team. In time it should be possible to eliminate those individuals who come into the service as a method of combatting their own unconscious anti-social tendencies, and gradually to establish among all grades of staff a new dignity and professional standing.

(12) Once this comes about it should ensure that the present rapid turnover of staff in these schools, which is so complicating a factor for the children, will be eliminated. At the moment the staff situation is much too fluid. One boy who had been in residence in a school for maladjusted children for only three years had had a succession of nine different teachers and eight different house-parents in his cottage.

It should be the aim of each school to establish a complete and well-trained staff who feel able to stay in the school indefinitely so that the boys are not constantly being thrown into a state of anxiety by shifting adult personnel. Some changes are, of course, inevitable, but it is virtually impossible for a child to feel secure in a community where the central adult figures are constantly leaving and being replaced. The reproduction of the family pattern is so essential an ingredient in the cure of these children that every change in staff affects one or more of them in much the same manner as would a divorce or separation in an ordinary home. Unless each staff member is able to understand the vital role he plays in the life of the children in his care, and the desperate attachments these children must establish, he has no place in the school.

Good staff relationships are equally to be desired – just as in a normal home the child can depend upon mutual trust and affection between the parents. One of the qualities which administrators and management committees must therefore look for in a headmaster particularly is his capacity to work harmoniously with his colleagues and establish 'a happy school'.

(**13**) From time to time I have emphasized the severe burden that this kind of work places on the individual staff-member. Not only has he to deal with seriously disturbed children but he is dealing with them all the time, day and night, and over repeated crises in the child's life. The strain is felt by every worker, but the chief weight falls on the shoulders of the headmaster and the residential staff. Casualties here are very high. House-parents resign because they feel at the end of their tether, teachers seek less onerous duties, headmasters have found their health broken under the strain. I am convinced that every effort should be made to ensure that very generous terminal leave is arranged for all staff. Without this relief the build-up of strain and anxiety becomes unbearable and results either in personal ill-health or in the development of defensive sadistic attitudes towards the children.

(**14**) The arduous nature of the work, and the resentment which emotionally disturbed and delinquent children build up in their environment, entices certain members of the staff to act towards the children in ways which cannot be excused on social, humanitarian, or psychological grounds. Here the educational inspectorate needs to keep an especially watchful eye. This question was one which attracted the attention of Dr Melitta Schmideberg[4] who attacked school inspectors with a vehemence which today seems extravagant. However, as she pointed out, inspectors are easily hoodwinked by ambitious and unscrupulous headmasters and house-matrons, and it is virtually impossible for an inspector to get a really accurate picture of a school situation with only occasional visits.

Inspectors are sometimes content merely to discuss problems in detail with the headmaster and pay scant attention to other members of the staff. The result is that many things go unseen. Other members of the staff are not willing to complain, partly out of a sense of loyalty but chiefly because they do not wish to risk their own chance of promotion.

It should prove of great advantage both to the school and the local authority if each school were supervised by an inspector who had himself had some clinical training and experience, otherwise it

4. Schmideberg, M., *Children in Need*. Allen & Unwin, 1948, p.100f.

is impossible for him to grasp the full significance of certain attitudes in staff members, or to calculate the effect of certain administrative decisions. I would further suggest that inspectors should live for a week or a fortnight each year in the school itself. In this way they would gain a more intimate knowledge of the children, of the various staff and their special aptitudes. This would also have the advantage of ensuring that the inspector came to be regarded by the staff not as a perambulating prying ogre, but as a deeply interested, informed, and familiar figure. I would support Melitta Schmideberg when she recommends that: 'Inspectors should have a first-class theoretical training, including modern methods of upbringing, psychology and social work, as well as practical experience of how to run an institution to treat children. They should be qualified to advise as well as criticize.'[5]

(15) Until such time as there are sufficient therapists and social workers to staff all these schools, it would seem prudent to place the younger children in schools which already possess full psychiatric services. Maladjustment and delinquency are easier to treat in the young and treatment is less prolonged. In this way we should be able to use what limited services we have to the best advantage.

(16) The ultimate aim must be to provide full psychiatric services in every school that caters for the seriously maladjusted child, even though many of the children may not themselves need psychotherapy. The existence in the school of a psychiatric unit brings about subtle changes in staff-attitudes, and helps to produce an environment in which therapy is possible for those children under treatment and recovery more likely for those who need only environmental handling. Evidence is building up which indicates that however warm, understanding, and imaginative an environment a school may be able to provide, poor results are obtained where there is no provision for psychotherapy.

(17) Not a few boys reach school-leaving age in a school for maladjusted children and are still incapable of normal life. They may, for instance, be orphans with no home to go to, or their home may be so rejective as to make it inadvisable for them to return there. Alternatively the psychotherapist may feel it essential that the child continue in treatment for some time. These children present a peculiar problem, for most of them are not able to fit easily into the ordinary type of working-boy's hostel. There is a need for a hostel

5. ibid. p.101.

which would cater for them especially. The headmasters and psychiatric staff of the schools from which the boys would be sent could keep in close touch with them and psychiatric treatment could be continued where necessary on a diminishing scale. As in other hostels the youths would work and pay for their keep.

Throughout this evaluation I have deliberately emphasized the social and communal aspects of maladjustment and delinquency. I have laid stress on the vital importance of the role these schools have to play in preventing emotionally disturbed children from becoming an incubus on society. What is not less important is the cost of maladjustment and anti-social attitudes to the disturbed child himself. He remains incapable of normal happiness in life; he will not be able to make a satisfying marriage; and he passes on to his children, in one form or another, the burden of his emotional disturbance.

On simple humanitarian grounds, therefore, we would emphasize, at the last, the value of treatment in helping these distressed youngers to take hold of life positively, creatively, and with some hope of personal integration. We should not limit our aims to the socially acceptable one of eradicating anti-social traits in the young. We should seek also by every means possible to help such children attain a normal life for themselves and their families, and to grasp a full measure of contentment and happiness.

17

Conclusion

No forward movement in human inquiry can be achieved without setting in motion a negative reaction. This is not to be regretted since it ensures that enthusiasts re-examine their premises and conclusions. It should be of value therefore, in summary, to enumerate some of the negative reactions which work of the kind we have done at Bredinghurst is likely to bring about.

First, there are those who complain that these schools attempt to treat boys who are too disturbed to be handled in an educational establishment and that a high proportion of maladjusted children should be in-patients in hospitals. Our experience shows, however, that the vast majority of maladjusted children can be treated successfully in an educational setting. It is better so. The hospitalized child housed in an artificial environment has few links with everyday experiences. The maladjusted child, however, is so near-normal over wide areas of his psychic constellation as to be traumatized by the clinical atmosphere of a hospital. In the main, hospitals are so organized that changes of medical and nursing staff take place constantly, thereby cutting across the development of transference relationships. The school, more easily than the hospital, can establish a normal setting for the child which duplicates as nearly as is possible the ordinary family setting.

Secondly, it is sometimes argued that working with a psychiatric team places too great a strain on the teacher. Against this we may set the fact that none of the teachers who worked in Bredinghurst over the period here reviewed has made such an allegation. Without exception they have contended that they prefer the alliance between education and psychiatry to 'working blind' in a school where there is no psychiatric unit. Too much can be made of the argument that psycho-analytical treatment disturbs the child and makes him more difficult to handle in class. The child who is not under treatment can be equally difficult. The child in treatment may regress to more primitive moods and modes of behaviour but he is at the same time gaining insight into himself and his motives. Consequently he may act out rather less than the child who is not in treatment. Violent, aggressive, and delinquent phases through which a boy in treatment may pass are likely to be comparatively short-lived.

No one suggests that treating, teaching, or managing the maladjusted child is an easy task for the staff. The real problem remains: How can we recruit into the service teachers of the requisite calibre?

This type of school offers society one last chance to cure the anti-social child. If this opportunity is not taken by each section of the staff the rate-payers might well ask if they are well served by their special schools.

Thirdly, it will be suggested that the psychiatric team over-complicates the problem: that re-education is a relatively simple procedure, and psychotherapy an unnecessarily intricate one. This attitude is surely no more than a reflection of society's discomfiture at discovering that maladjustment is not merely the result of a moral twist in the mind. In these circumstances, as Bovet[1] suggests, the re-educator is inclined to take refuge more than ever in classical and superficial methods, because simple and anxiety-free conceptions reassure him and *lull him in the false conviction that he understands all there is need to know*. The point of tension here between the re-educator and the therapist is that the educator wants to teach, and the therapist hopes to learn.

Fourthly, there are those who will oppose the employment of a psychiatric team on the grounds that 'psycho-analysis is an inexact science'. Most of these critics know little about psycho-analysis and fail to realize just how exact a science it is over wide areas of human behaviour, and that it is precise enough to be able to detect many of the gross errors which are commonly made in child management. Psychiatry, since it is dealing with human beings and not invariables like time or distance, must to some extent be inexact. But in the treatment of the maladjusted child it is infinitely more exact than is education – the only suggested alternative.

Fifthly, some educationists fear that if a psychiatric team are at work in a school they will wish to 'dictate' to the rest of the staff

1. *Juvenile Delinquency*, World Health Organisation, Geneva, 1951.

how to handle the children in their care. This is a false assessment of the manner in which the therapeutic process bears on the school. The psychiatrist relies not upon dictatorial edicts, but places his confidence in the inherent dynamic in psycho-analysis as a persuasive force. In fact, the most constant complaint which has been levelled at the psychiatric team in Bredinghurst is that we have been loath to instruct other members of the staff on how to handle individual children. We have always contended that to do so would be presumptious on our part since we do not have the day-to-day care of the child, and since each adult can act constructively only from his personal endowment and conviction.

Finally, it may be argued that a psychiatric team could undermine the discipline of a school. It is true, of course, that severe corporal punishment, gross humiliation and ridicule of a child and certain other disciplinary techniques are inimical to emotional health, and a psychiatrist might well feel bound to raise such matters with the headmaster if they occurred. In general, however, therapy can only be achieved within a disciplined environment. Constructive discipline does not mean severe repressive measures, regimentation, or obsessional rules of order and hygiene. It is a matter of the personality of the adult; of example, not chastisement. Good discipline depends basically on a healthy relationship between child and adult. That a school may have a long list of rules and regulations is no indication that it is well disciplined. The teacher who needs to rely on implicit obedience, threats, and verbal or physical assault to gain compliance has failed to build up that affective relationship with the child which makes effective discipline possible.

Postscript

This book has been written in the present tense as though Bredinghurst still existed as I have described it. In fact it no longer does. For reasons which were wholly outside our control the school was restructured in such a way as to make our style of work impossible. One unfortunate consequence of the termination of the experiment is that it has not been possible for us to undertake the long-term follow-up study we had planned and which would, we feel, have added weight to our argument.

Until recently virtually all the pioneer and research work in the treatment of maladjustment had been carried on in private or independent schools. In these schools one outstandingly gifted individual has built around himself a therapeutic environment and a treatment team, and has attempted to conceptualize and communicate his methods and technique (Lyward, Dockar-Drysdale, Lennhoff). There are a number of reasons why this superlative work should have been achieved outside the State system, not the least being the fact that the school could function free from the domination of local authority committees and officers who might lack the knowledge and skill necessary to understand the rationale of the treatment situation. We were fortunate in Bredinghurst in that for ten years we were able to work within the State system and remain comparatively free to work in our own way.

We, on the psychiatric side, benefited from working so closely with the educational and child-care staff, and though our association is now at an end, it is heartening to reflect that other schools and other local authorities are adopting very similar methods, and that among sensitive and aware administrators we have found wide support. I am convinced that as local authorities throughout the country become familiar with the research that is now going on in this difficult field many more schools will be established very much after the pattern I have tried to outline.

Bibliography

ALEXANDER, F. and STAUB., *The Criminal, the Judge and the Public*, Allen & Unwin, London, 1931
ABRAHAM, K., *Selected Papers on Psycho-Analysis*, Hogarth, London, 1927
AICHHORN, A., *Wayward Youth*, Imago, London, 1925

BENNETT, I., *Delinquent and Neurotic Children*, Tavistock, London, 1960
BETTLEHEIM, B., *Love is Not Enough*, Allen & Unwin, London, 1952
  Truants From Life, The Free Press, Chicago, 1955
  and SYLVESTER, E., 'A Therapeutic Milieu', *American Journal of Orthopsychiatry*, Vol. XVIII, 1948
BIDDLE, S., 'The Use of Transference in Dealing with Delinquents', *American Journal of Orthopsychiatry*, Vol. III, 1933
BOVET, L., *Juvenile Delinquency*, World Health Organization, Geneva, 1951
BOWLBY, J., *Forty-Four Juvenile Thieves*, Bailliere, London, 1944
  Maternal Care and Mental Health, World Health Organization, Geneva, 1951
  and ROBERTSON, J. and ROSENBLUTH, D., 'A Two-Year-Old Goes to Hospital', *The Psychoanalytic Study of the Child*, Vol. VII, Imago, London, 1952
BRONNER, A. F. and HEALY, W., *Delinquents and Criminals*, Macmillan, New York, 1925
  and HEALY, W., *New Light on Delinquency and its Treatment*, Yale University Press, New Haven, 1936
BURLINGHAM, D. and FREUD, A., *Young Children in Wartime: A Year's Work in a Residential War Nursery*, Allen & Unwin, London, 1942
BURN, M., *Mr Lyward's Answer*, Hamish Hamilton, London, 1956
BURT, C., *The Young Delinquent*, University of London Press, 1925

COMFORT, A., *Authority and Delinquency in the Modern State*, Routledge and Kegan Paul, London, 1950

DOCKAR-DRYSDALE, B. E., 'The Residential Treatment of "Frozen" Children', *British Journal of Delinquency*, Vol. IX, 1958

EISSLER, K. R., 'General Problems of Delinquency', in *Searchlights on Delinquency*, Imago, London, 1949

FENICHEL, O., *The Psychoanalytic Theory of Neurosis*, Norton, New York, 1945
FERENCZI, S., 'The Unwelcome Child and his Death Instinct', *International Journal of Psycho-Analysis*, Vol. IX, 1929
FLUGEL, J. C., *The Psychoanalytic Study of the Family*, Hogarth, London, 1921
FREUD, A., *The Ego and Mechanisms of Defence*, Hogarth, London, 1937
  'Aggression in Relation to Emotional Development; Normal and Pathological', *The Psychoanalytic Study of the Child*, Vol. III–IV, Imago, London, 1947
  The Psychoanalytic Treatment of Children, Imago, London, 1946
  'Emotional and Instinctive Development', in *Child Health and Development*, Ed. by Prof. R. W. B. Ellis, John Churchill, London, 1947
  'Some Remarks on Infant Observation', *The Psychoanalytic Study of the Child*, Vol. VIII, Imago, London, 1953
  'Problems of Infantile Neurosis: a Discussion', *The Psychoanalytic Study of the Child*, Vol. IX, Imago, London, 1954
  and BURLINGHAM, D., *Young Children in Wartime: a Year's Work in a Residential War Nursery*, Allen & Unwin, London, 1942
FREUD, S., *Three Essays on the Theory of Sexuality*, Hogarth, London, 1905
  Instincts and their Vicissitudes, Hogarth, London, 1915
  Mourning and Melancholia, Hogarth, London, 1917
  Inhibitions, Symptoms and Anxiety, Hogarth, London, 1926
  Moses and Monotheism, Hogarth, London, 1939
FRIEDLANDER, K., 'Formation of the Antisocial Character', *The Psychoanalytic Study of the Child*, Vol. I, Imago, London, 1945
  The Psychoanalytical Approach to Juvenile Delinquency, Kegan Paul, London, 1947
  'Latent Delinquency and Ego Development', in *Searchlights on Delinquency*, Ed. by K. R. Eissler, Imago, London, 1949
  'Neurosis and Home Background: a Preliminary Report', *The Psychoanalytic Study of the Child*, Vol. III–IV, Imago, London, 1949
FURER, M. and MAHLER, M. S., 'The Symbiotic Syndrome of Infantile Psychosis', *Psychoanalytic Quarterly*, Vol. XXIX
FYVEL, T. R., *The Insecure Offenders*, Chatto & Windus, London, 1961

GLOVER, E., Notes on Oral Character Formation', *International Journal of Psycho-Analysis*, Vol. VI, 1925
  'Outline of the Investigation and Treatment of Delinquency in Great Britain', in *Searchlights on Delinquency*, Ed. by K. R. Eissler, Imago, London, 1949
  Psycho-Analysis and Child Psychiatry, Imago, London, 1953
  The Roots of Crime, Imago, London, 1960
GLUECK, S. and GLUECK, E. T., *One Thousand Juvenile Delinquents*, Harvard University Press, Cambridge, Mass., 1934
GREENACRE, P., 'The Predisposition to Anxiety', in *Trauma, Growth and Personality*, Hogarth, London, 1941
  'Conscience in the Psychopath', *American Journal of Orthopsychiatry*, Vol. XV, 1945

'Problems of Infantile Neurosis; a Discussion', *The Psychoanalytic Study of the Child*, Vol. IX, Imago, London, 1954

HARTMANN, H. and KRIS, E., 'The Genetic Approach in Psychoanalysis', *The Psychoanalytic Study of the Child*, Vol. I, Imago, London, 1945
HEALY, W., *The Individual Delinquent*, Heinemann, London, 1915
and BRONNER, A. F., *Delinquents and Criminals*, Macmillan, New York, 1925
and ALEXANDER, F., *The Roots of Crime: Psychoanalytic Studies*, Knopf, New York and London, 1935
and BRONNER, A. F., *New Light on Delinquency and its Treatment*, Yale University Press, New Haven, 1936
HEIMANN, P., 'On Counter-Transference', *International Journal of Psycho-Analysis*, Vol. XXXI, 1950
'Dynamics and Transference Interpretation', *International Journal of Psycho-Analysis*, Vol. XXXVIII, 1956
and KLEIN, M. and MONEY-KYRLE, R., *Developments in Psycho-Analysis*, Tavistock, 1952
HOFFER, W., 'Deceiving the Deceiver', in *Searchlights on Delinquency*, Ed. by K. R. Eissler, Imago, London, 1949
Psycho-Analysis, Williams and Wilkins, Baltimore, 1949

JONES, H., *Reluctant Rebels*, Tavistock, London, 1960

KLEIN, M., 'The Development of a Child', *International Journal of Psycho-Analysis*, Vol. IV, 1923
'The Role of the School in the Libidinal Development of the Child', *International Journal of Psycho-Analysis*, Vol. V., 1924
'On Child Analysis', *International Journal of Psycho-Analysis*, Vol. VIII, 1927
The Psycho-Analysis of Children, Hogarth, London, 1932
Contributions to Psycho-Analysis, Hogarth, London, 1948
and RIVIERE, J., 'Love, Hate and Reparation', *Psycho-Analytical Epitomes*, No. 2, Hogarth, London, 1936
and HEIMANN, P. and MONEY-KYRLE, R., *Developments in Psycho-Analysis*, Tavistock, London, 1952
KRIS, E., and HARTMANN, H., 'The Genetic Approach in Psychoanalysis', *The Psychoanalytic Study of the Child*, Vol. I, Imago, London, 1945

LENNHOFF, F. G., *Exceptional Children*, Allen & Unwin, London, 1960

MAHLER, M. S., 'On Child Psychosis and Schizophrenia', *The Psychoanalytic Study of the Child*, Vol. VII, Imago, London, 1954
and FURER, M., 'The Symbiotic Syndrome of Infantile Psychosis', *Psychoanalytic Quarterly*, Vol. XXIX.
MANNHEIM, H., *Juvenile Delinquency in an English Middletown*, Kegan Paul, London, 1948
MIDDLEMORE, M. P., *The Nursing Couple*, Hamish Hamilton, London, 1941
MILNER, M., 'A Suicidal Symptom in a Child of Three', *International Journal of Psycho-Analysis*, Vol. XXV, 1944

MONEY-KYRLE, R. and KLEIN, M. and HEIMANN, P., *Developments in Psycho-Analysis*, Tavistock, London, 1952

MULLINS, *Crime and Psychology*, Methuen, London, 1943
Why Crime, Methuen, London, 1945

NEIL, A. S., *The Problem Child*, Jenkins, London, 1929

NUNBERG, H., 'The Sense of Guilt and the Need for Punishment', *International Journal of Psycho-Analysis*, Vol. VII, 1926

REDL, F. and WINEMAN, D., *Children Who Hate*, The Free Press, Glencoe, III, 1951
Controls From Within, The Free Press, Glencoe, III, 1952

RIVIERE, J. and KLEIN, M., 'Love, Hate and Reparation', *Psychoanalytic Epitomes*, No. 2, Hogarth, London, 1937

ROBERTSON, J. and BOWLBY, J. and ROSENBLUTH, D., 'A Two-Year-Old Goes to Hospital', *Psychoanalytic Study of the Child*, Vol. VII, Imago, London, 1952

ROSENBLUTH, D., and ROBERTSON, J. and BOWLBY, J., 'A Two-Year-Old Goes to Hospital', *The Psychoanalytic Study of the Child*, Vol. VII, Imago, London, 1952

STEKEL, W., *Sadism and Masochism*, Liveright, New York, 1929

STERN, M. M., 'Infantile Trauma', *International Journal of Psycho-Analysis*, Vol. XXXVIII, 1956

STOTT, D. H., *Delinquency and Human Nature*, Carnegie United Dominion Trust, Dunfermline, 1950

SYLVESTER, E. and BETTLEHEIM, B., 'A Therapeutic Milieu', *American Journal of Orthopsychiatry*, Vol. XVIII, 1948

WATSON, J. A. F., *The Child and the Magistrate*, Cape, London, 1942

WHITE, W. A., *Insanity and the Criminal Law*, Macmillan, New York, 1923

WINNICOTT, D. W., *Clinical Notes on Disorders of Childhood*, Heinemann, London, 1931
'Stealing and Telling Lies', in *The Child and the Family*, Tavistock, London, 1957
'Residential Management as Treatment for Difficult Children', 'Breast Feeding', 'Aggression', 'The Impulse to Steal', and 'Some Psychological Aspects of Juvenile Delinquency', in *The Child and the Outside World*, Tavistock, London, 1957
'Reparation in Respect of Mother's Organized Defence Against Depression', 'Anxiety Associated with Insecurity', 'Primitive Emotional Development', 'Hate in the Countertransference', 'Psychoses and Child Care', 'Withdrawal and Regression', and 'The Antisocial Tendency', in *Collected Papers*, Tavistock, London, 1958

ZILBOORG, G., *The Psychology of the Criminal Act and Punishment*, Tavistock, London, 1954

ADDITIONAL BIBLIOGRAPHY FOR THE SECOND EDITION

ALLEN, F. H., *Psychotherapy with Children*, Kegan Paul, 1948
ALT, H. *Residential Treatment for the Disturbed Child*, Bailey Bros. & Swinfen, 1960
AXLINE, V. M., *Dibs in Search of Self*, Gollancz, 1966

BALBERNIE,, R. *Residential Work with Children*, Pergamon, 1966
BETTELHEIN, B., *The Empty Fortress*, Free Press, 1967
BLOS, P., *On Adolescence*, Free Press, 1962

ERIKSON, E. H., *Identity*, Faber, 1968

GINNOTT, H., *Group Psychotherapy with Children*, McGraw-Hill, 1961
GOFFMAN, E., *Asylums*, Doubleday, 1959

HALMOS, P., *The Faith of the Counsellors*, Constable, 1965
HOOD, R., *Borstal Re-assessed*, Heinemann, 1965

KAHN, J. H. and NURSTEN, J. P., *Unwillingly to School*, Pergamon, 1964

LORENZ, K., *On Aggression*, Methuen, 1966
LYND, H. M., *On Shame and the Search for Identity*, Routledge, 1958

MURPHY, L. B., *Widening World of Childhood*, Basic Books, 1962

OPIE, P. and I., *The Lore and Language of School Children*, O.U.P., 1964

SLAVSON, S. R., *Reclaiming the Delinquent*, Macmillan, 1965
STORR, A., *Human Aggression*, Allen Lane, 1968
  Integrity of the Personality, Penguin, 1963

WINNICOTT, D. W., *The Family and Individual Development*, Tavistock, 1965
  The Maturational Process and the Facilitating Environment, Hogarth, 1965

Index

ACTING OUT:
   in school, 45
   in next generation, 156
   in stealing, 119
Administrators, 17
   and psychotherapy, 97–8, 170–1
   and selection of staff, 174–5
Aggression, 39–41
   and anxiety, 65–6, 128
   oral, 141
   physical, 128–31
Aichhorn, A., 54, 125, 126–7, 146
Alexander, F., 158, 159
Ambivalence:
   in child, 160
   in parents, 36
Anger, 66
Anti-social child, 54, 101–11, 160–2
   and despair, 78
   and hope, 89
   and stealing, 118–20
Anxiety, 20
   and dependence, 49
   and discipline, 45
   and family, 161
   and running away, 25
   in staff, 127
   in treatment, 61

BACKWARDNESS, 27
Bettleheim, B., 126, 146
Bovet, L., 173, 174, 180
Bowlby, J., 161, 168
Bullying, 59–60, 67–8
Breast, 109
Bredinghurst:
   the school, 23–31
   method, 32–52

CASTRATION, 69, 86

Child-care staff, 46
   parent-surrogates, 29–31, 46, 49
   qualities needed in, 95, 171–4
Child Guidance Services, 13, 20, 21, 26, 33, 55
City: setting for school, 24–6, 170
Classes: Numerical size, 36, 172
Confession, 105, 107, 118–20
Communication, 78–84
Conference, 36–8, 51, 78, 81
Conscience, *see also* super-ego, 43–4
Cottage system, 23
   family basis of, 29–30, 171
Courts, juvenile, 35, 98–9, 112–21
Crying, 40, 106, 127, 140

DEFENCE MECHANISMS, 28, 61, 64, 70, 73, 104, 153, 162, 163
Defiance, 70
Delinquency, 54, 101–11, 147, 158–9
Dependence, 19, 42, 49
Depression, 28, 144
Deprivation, 101, 122, 160–1, 166
Despair, 71, 153
Destructiveness, 66, 70
Discipline, 28, 61–2, 63–77
   and psychotherapy, 181
   as therapeutic technique, 15–17, 20, 103, 162
   lax, 20, 63, 97
   need of, 45–6
   self-, 65
Disillusionment, 131
Dockar-Drysdale, B. E., 126

EDUCATION, 27–9, 172
Eissler, K. R., 146, 164
Encopresis, 124, 132
Enuresis, 50, 124, 149, 155
Environment:

and trauma, 161
distrust of, 162,
failure of, 123, 153
school, 23–52, 103, 109, 122, 163

FALSE SELF, 54, 136
Family, 24–5, 161
  cottage as, 29
Fantasy, 45, 118–19, 160
  unconscious, 43–5
Fear, 77
Finance, 30–1, 172–3
Follow-up, 51–2
Freud, A., 69, 146, 160, 163
Freud, A., and Burlingham, D., 46–8
Freud, S., 125, 159, 161
Friedlander, K., 146
Fury, 66

GANGS, 160
Glover, E., 97, 146, 159
Gratitude, 20, 59, 88
Guilt, 54, 66, 148
  in anti-social child, 101–11
  in parents, 34, 96
  unconscious, 43, 73, 159

HALLUCINATIONS, 159
Hate, 91, 126, 165
  in love relationship, 65–6
  in regression, 148
Headmaster, 23, 36, 51, 93–4, 98, 176
Health, 23
Healy, W., and Bronner, F. A., 54
Heimann, P., 67
Hoffer, W., 164
Home:
  and school, 24–6
  disturbed, 34, 56–7
  school as, 27, 170–1
Homosexuality, 72, 174, 176–7
Hope, 56–8, 70, 89, 90, 103, 110
Hostels, 51, 177–8
Humiliation, 72, 96

IDENTIFICATION, 160
Inspectors, 98, 136, 176–7
Integration, 61, 125, 163, 178
  and withdrawn state, 134
Intellectualisation, 27
Intelligence, 27, 172
Introjection, 162

JEALOUSY AND ENVY, 41, 47, 92, 94, 127

KHAN, M. R., 13
Klein, M., 89, 146, 159

LOSS, 132, 158, 161

MADNESS, 34, 56, 58
Magic, 159–60
Magistrates, 98–9, 112–21
Mahler, M. S., and Furer, M., 127
Maladjustment, 53–62, 158–67
Management, 122, 166
Manic defence, 28
Manners, 88, 123–4
Masturbation, 86–7
Meals, 87–8, 123
Moral attitudes, 16–18, 71–2, 163, 165
  to stealing, 103, 107–8
Mother, 109, 160–1, 164
Mourning, 133
Murder, 127–8, 130, 148

NEIL, A. S., 63
Nicknames, 123

ŒDIPUS COMPLEX, 65, 139
Omnipotence, 147, 159–60

PAIN, 42, 104–5, 109–10, 131
Parental role:
  headmaster in, 94
  psychotherapist in, 125–6
  staff in, 29, 46–8, 124, 171
  State in, 31
Parents, 24–6, 30, 33–5, 45, 50, 57
  and rejection, 147–8
  and psychotherapy, 96–7
Permissiveness, 18–20, 63, 71, 77, 163
Physical contact:
  in transference, 127–44
  with mother, 148
Privacy, 132–4
Probation service, 98
Psychiatric social worker, 33–4, 51, 154
Psycho-analysis, 18, 44, 93–100, 158–67, 179–81
Psychosis, 149–50, 154, 159, 172
Psychotherapy, 49, 57–62, 64, 82, 165–7
  appreciation of, 179–80
  distrust of, 93–100
  law, 112–21

objections to, 179–81
school setting for, 55, 158–67, 177
Punishment, 46
  and parents, 97
  self-, 107

RAGE: 65–6, 68–9
  and anti-social child, 126–7
  and control, 130
  and despair, 67
  and destructiveness, 129
Reality, 118–20, 159
Reality-testing, 48, 77
Redl, F., and Wineman, D., 146
Regression, 19, 163
  anal, 108–9, 123–4
  and withdrawn states, 134
  in transference, 41–2, 108–9
  oral, 123
  psycho-physical, 146–8
Reich, W., 158
Rejection:
  and hate, 126
  and moral attitudes, 71–2
  by mother, 161
  through illness, 80, 128
  self-preservation, 147–8
Reparation, 58
Repression, 61
Restitution, 43, 58–9, 101–11, 126, 131, 161–2
Retribution, 161
Roles, 83–4, 91–2
Running away, 25–6, 35, 39–40, 74–7, 85–6
Ruthlessness, 66

SADO-MASOCHISM, 59
  and the delinquent, 101, 103
  and the moralist, 72
  and the teacher, 174
Schmideberg, M., 146, 176, 177
School:
  Bredinghurst, 15–52
  a home, 170–1
  not a hospital, 26, 169–70, 179
  'outside', 27
Security, 45, 54, 64–5
Selection:
  of children, 33, 172
  of staff, 173–5
Self-control, 66, 74, 109
Self-cure, 104, 163

Sentimentality, 28, 56, 70–1
Sexuality, 86–7
  stimulation, 92
  bisexuality, 160
Sibling rivalry, 41, 59
  and anti-social child, 127
  and neurotic, 160
Splitting, 28, 54, 161, 162, 164
Staff, 43, 60–1
  changes in, 175–6
  selection in, 173–5
Staff relationships:
  communication, 78–82
  tensions, 21, 32, 85–92
Stanton, A. H., and Schwartz, M. S., 48–9, 56–7
Staub, H., 159
Stealing, 102
  and hope, 89–90
  and the court, 112–21
  and regression, 124
Stern, M. M., 161, 162
Suicidal fantasies, 60, 80, 139–40, 148
Super-ego, 17, 158–9, 161
  sadistic, 103, 159, 162
Supplementary ego, 42, 67, 69
Swearing, 81, 86, 123
Symptoms, 17, 33, 74, 159

TEACHERS, 27–9, 130, 170
  training and selection, 173–4
Testing out, 38, 70, 75, 136
Threats, 71, 158
Training:
  of inspectors, 176–7
  of teachers, 173
Transference, 17, 20, 21, 59–60, 82, 141
  and aggressions, 128–31, 141–2
  in treatment, 125, 148
Trauma, 147–8, 160–1

VIOLENCE, 60, 127–31

WEANING, 145, 147
Winnicott, D. W., 54, 58, 74, 88, 90, 94, 101, 102, 108, 110, 114, 122, 125, 134, 146, 151, 161
Withdrawn states:
  and regression, 131, 134
  in the mother, 148
Working through, 144–5

ZILBOORG, G., 104–7